COACH MANJU NITTA'S BASEBALL SECRETS

MICHAEL M. OKIHIRO

AuthorHouse™
1663 Liberty Drive
Bloomington, IN 47403
www.authorhouse.com
Phone: 1-800-839-8640

First published by AuthorHouse   3/30/2011

ISBN: 978-1-4567-6218-6 (e)
ISBN: 978-1-4567-6219-3 (sc)

Library of Congress Control Number: 2011906811

Printed in the United States of America

Any people depicted in stock imagery provided by Thinkstock are models, and such images are being used for illustrative purposes only. Certain stock imagery © Thinkstock.

This book is printed on acid-free paper.

Because of the dynamic nature of the Internet, any web addresses or links contained in this book may have changed since publication and may no longer be valid. The views expressed in this work are solely those of the author and do not necessarily reflect the views of the publisher, and the publisher hereby disclaims any responsibility for them.

BOOK DESIGN: Mele Johnson and Michele Okihiro

COVER DRAWING BY: Jill Okihiro

TABLE OF CONTENTS

FORWARD

LES MURAKAMI

COACH OF THE UNIVERSITY OF HAWAII
RAINBOW BASEBALL TEAM FROM 1971-2000

George "Manju" Nitta is a friend with a great love of baseball. He supported me in my early years while I was coaching at the University of Hawaii and came to many of our Rainbow games during the "bleacher" years. My family remembers him telling them jokes and making them laugh.

Years later I found out that Manju had found his calling in teaching the youth of Hawaii the basics of baseball, with passion. He has spent countless hours over many, many years teaching youngsters the fundamentals of the sport. He does this because of his great love for baseball and enjoyment watching his students improve and excel through the years.

Coach Les Murakami
Honolulu Star Bulletin Photo

I'm glad someone finally decided to write about the amazing and generous, George "Manju" Nitta who has given so freely of his time to the youth of our community without any compensation in return.

INTRODUCTION

This is an informational book on the basic mechanics of baseball, how to throw, field and hit a baseball. The same basic mechanics apply to softball. They are easy to learn and by learning them, the game should become more enjoyable and exciting. The information is aimed primarily at youngsters who are learning the game, but should find application to ballplayers at every stage of development.

As every serious student of baseball knows, there are dozens of instructional books on the game. So why another one? Well, there are a number of us who feel that George "Manju" Nitta's knowledge of the intricacies of the game goes far beyond the obvious and ordinary, and that many of the things that he has learned and has been willing to teach, his *secrets,* are not found in the many books that are available today. Furthermore, he says he's learned so much from the kids as well as the parents who bring them to him and some of these insights will be included in this book.

Manju first learned his baseball by copying and imitating his heroes and his heroes were the stars of the championship Waipahu Americans of Japanese Ancestry (AJA) and Rural Red Sox teams who roamed Hans L'Orange Field in Waipahu in the late 40s and 50s. Copying and imitating baseball stars is an excellent way of learning the game, but baseball is a fast game and many of the nuances of the game are hard to see and easily lost in the quickness and speed of the game. Copying and imitating is not the easiest way to learn the game.

Nevertheless, Manju became an excellent ballplayer. He took part in the highest echelon of local baseball in Hawaii and played professionally in Japan for a couple of years. After his playing days were over, he managed and coached the Ujimori Hawks in the Hawaii Baseball League (HBL) for another ten years. However, by his own admission, he was not a good coach and, in fact, says he was the meanest coach in the islands.

It was only after he "retired" from baseball that he began to really learn baseball. He began "*mind-picking*" the greats of baseball including Mr. Francis Funai who had a legacy of teaching baseball basics. But over the years, it was Mr. Stanley Hashimoto who became his "*Sensei,*" his teacher, counselor and advisor.

Along the way, and with his *Sensei's* help, Manju began the process of "*breaking down*" the intricacies of the game into its component parts and putting them back in the proper sequence. He spent many hours in front of a huge mirror that covers one entire wall in his living room, going through the motions and movements involved in baseball, discovering the intricacies of the game, breaking down each act of baseball into its component parts. He found that when these components come together sequentially, smoothly and swiftly, that's when you'll see baseball as the beautiful game that it is.

Subsequently, Manju has picked up on Mr. Funai's legacy of teaching youngsters of all ages the basics of baseball. Manju holds baseball clinics every Sunday afternoon from January through November. And before the start of every baseball season, he gives dozens of clinics to teams and leagues who call on him annually and the numbers keep increasing all the time. His clinics are free and he has not made a dime for the thousands of hours he has spent with the ballplayers.

Mr. Funai died in 1999 and although there are many ball players who still remember some of his lessons, what he had taught will probably soon be gone. Manju has taught and continues to teach many youngsters, but we felt that he needed something in a book form as a means of continuing his legacy and reaching more kids. As his daughter Misty has said, "He has such a passion for the game, and so much to share," and what he has to share has no time limits as long as the game of baseball continues.

In his clinics, he never says that his is the only way to throw a baseball or his is the only was to hit a ball. However, he has found that his methods have been successful. No question, others have different ways, and still others may find better ways, and that is great.

Perhaps the essence of his methods is his belief that the player himself has to *acquire the feeling*, the indescribable sensory feedback after making the catch, the good throw or the solid base hit. After all, it's not teaching that's important, it's the *learning* by the kids. So he tells his coaches and assistants not to go grabbing the kids and telling them you're not doing this or that. Instead, he shows them the drills that are needed to correct the faults. His philosophy is to let the kids be free and they'll correct themselves until they get the "*feeling*." Then they've learned what he's been trying to teach.

Some of the terms that he uses are uniquely Manju's and need to be defined, but they are fairly explainable, very catchy and easy to remember.

So this is what we intend to do here -- to put down in words and pictures what Manju teaches every Sunday in his baseball clinics. There is no way that we can do complete justice to him because his very presence in the drills, his laughter, his jokes, his mannerisms, and especially his enthusiasm that make the clinics so successful, are impossible to put into a printed form. But this is our attempt. We will try.

And always remember Manju's mantra which has been this: *Have fun because this is baseball.*

DEDICATION

This book is dedicated to two men, both deceased, who were instrumental in Coach Manju's maturation and devotion to teaching and coaching baseball.

STANLEY SEISO HASHIMOTO
(1932-2000)

Stan Hashimoto was a great baseball player out of Waipahu High School who also played for the University of Hawaii (U.H.), the Rural Red Sox, and in the Japanese Professional League. He could hit a baseball as few others could, with lots of power. Throughout his career he was invariably the clean-up batter of whatever team he played for. In 1954 the noted sports writer Carl Machado called him, "the best first baseman in the Isles."

In his first year at U.H. he led the

Stan Hashimoto
Photo by Phillip S. Yano

Rainbows from his position at first base to the championship of the Winter Baseball League and was awarded an "Oscar" as the top player of the team. He was the captain of the Rainbows during his junior and senior years. After his senior year in 1954 he was voted on the NCAA District 8 All-Star Team.

During the same period, he was playing first base for Waipahu in the AJA Senior League and the Rural Red Sox in the Hawaii League. While he was playing for them, the Rural Red Sox won the Hawaii League championship for a record seven years in a row, from 1950-56. In 1952, and again in 1953, Hashimoto was voted the Most Valuable Player of the Territorial AJA Tournaments.

In 1957 he began a five year journey in the Japanese Professional Baseball League, the first four with the Toei Flyers and the last with Taiyo Whales. His cumulative batting average for the five years was a respectable .261.

He returned to Hawaii in 1961, resumed teaching in the public school system, and coached baseball at McKinley High School for a few years. He eventually went into the insurance business but maintained a strong interest in sports, especially in martial arts. He attained the black belt in both *aikido* and *kendo*, the principles of which he felt were very important in all sports.

A complex man with strong convictions, he usually refused requests for advice in baseball or assistance in coaching. These included requests from former teammates. Thus some felt that he was aloof and conceited which was far from the truth.

At age 42, George Manju Nitta sought out this childhood baseball hero of his to learn more about the game. Their first encounter was confrontational and almost disastrous for Manju, but over the years they developed a mutual respect that grew with time. Subsequently Manju continually sought Stan's wise counseling and Stan became Manju's honorable *"Sensei"* until his death in 2000.

FRANCIS AKIYOSHI FUNAI
(1907-1999)

Even the University of Hawaii's Rainbow Coach Les Murakami used to call him "Coach." Francis Funai has been called the best baseball mind in Hawaii. Even when he was nearing ninety years of age, he was still sought to counsel youngsters in the fundamentals and details of the game that has been part of him since he first learned to love the sport while growing up in Waialua.

Although he played for Mid-Pacific Institute from where he graduated in 1927, it was at St. Louis High School that he began to make a name for himself. He first went to St. Louis as an assistant to Charley "Fat" Fernandez and together, they guided the Crusaders to five championships in six seasons, from 1936-41. Funai became the head coach in 1943, retired in 1959, but was re-hired from 1967-70. He guided the Crusaders to nine championships during his 20 or so years at St. Louis, including four consecutive championships from 1945 to '48.

A Young Francis Funai
Funai Family Collection

But that is hardly the end of the story. He was asked to be the pitching coach at Iolani by Les Uyehara. Then Mel Seki asked for his help at Pearl City High School. He helped Les Murakami at the Rainbow baseball clinics. And for many years he held free weekend clinics every fall at McKinley High School.

throw the ball, how to field grounders, how to hold the bat, etc. He spent countless hours going over and over baseball fundamentals during practice sessions, the infrastructure upon which to build.

And through all the years he has never stopped learning and loving the game. "I'm always looking for new ideas," he said. "The more you know the more situations you can deal with."

Dick Kashiwaeda, the former Asahi and Tokyo Giants third baseman, assisted Funai at many of his clinics. He says that Funai always studied the real good ball players, tried to analyze what they did that made them stand out over the crowd. He would study and learn their mechanics and, on the ball field and at his clinics, he tried to teach his players the steps necessary to make them quicker, stronger, faster and consistent winners. He was always a step or two ahead of the rest.

The late Mel Seki, teacher, principal and Pearl City High coach, played for Funai at St. Louis and remained close to him. Seki absorbed most of his teachings and says that, "Mr. Funai never stopped learning." Seki also added that, "His main purpose was not just to teach boys to become ball players but to teach them to become men. He believed in building character along with baseball skills and felt that it was the coach's responsibility to field a first rate club of gentlemen ball players."

Francis Funai has been called "a guru," "a baseball genius," "a coach's coach," "one of a kind," "a legend." He was all of these.

BATTING

Everything is done by "feelings." You've got to make the kid taste it, make the kid feel it. You can't just tell the kid that this is the way to throw a ball or hit a ball. He's got to taste how good it is, to feel how good it is to throw the ball right or whack the ball solidly. And when the kid starts throwing harder and hitting harder, he's going to change because he wants that "feeling."

I tell parents and coaches, don't go grabbing the kids too much. Let them do it on their own because they're going to correct themselves. Just encourage. If you hold them too much and keep telling them, "Do this," and "Do that," they're going to get stuck. Let them be free.

The great Ted Williams said that, "Hitting a baseball is the single most difficult thing to do in sports." But he also has said that, "Hitting can be improved at almost any level. If there is such a thing as a science in sport, hitting a baseball is it. It is not an exact science. As with any science, there are fundamentals."

Another legendary baseball star Roger Hornsby said: "A great hitter isn't born, he's made. He's made out of practice, fault correction and confidence." Coach Manju also feels strongly that hitting can be learned by acquiring certain basic fundamentals of baseball and doing a lot of repetitions. He says that we can't all be homerun sluggers, but we can all become good hitters.

This confirms Marv Bittinger's belief that, "Disciplined hitters are best developed with patient coaching."

BATTING FORM AND STANCE

The batting form and stance can vary but it's probably best to start with a square stance, feet about shoulder width apart, knees and hips slightly bent and weight on the balls of the feet.

Square Stance

HOLDING THE BAT

The bat should be held with the small knuckles (also called the middle knuckles or the proximal inter-phalangeal joints) of the right hand in line with the small knuckles of the left.

Line up the Small
(Middle Knuckles)

If you line up the big knuckles, your shoulders and arms will become "locked" and you will not be able to snap your wrists at the ball. The grip should be firm and tension free, but not tight. (The last three fingers of the hands are the strongest in gripping anything.)

No! Not the Big
Knuckles

The lower hand should not butt against the knob of the bat. If the lower hand is held against the knob, the twisting action of the bat may produce blisters or may cut into the hand. Another less popular option is to hold the bat with the lower hand over the knob of the bat.

Don't Butt the Knob

Then we "measure" to be sure that the bat can reach the opposite edge of the plate. You should be able to touch the other side of the plate with the bat in your left (front) hand.

Measure

The bat is held up above the back shoulder with both hands about the level of your eyes, so you can pull the bat down and across your chest for a down-plane swing. The fat part of the bat should be leaning toward the pitcher and not toward the catcher. The head should be straight up so that the batter has a clear view of the ball as it comes towards him. The elbows should be pointing downward and comfortably apart. Keeping the front elbow tucked in and back will facilitate easy balance.

Ready or Launch Position

This is the "ready and balanced position". From here the ballplayer should practice swinging the bat with full force, the way he or she wants to hit a ball, and then resume the batting or launch position form while looking at the pitcher before the ball is thrown.

3

READY AND BALANCED POSITION FOR HITTING

With a bat in his hands and in a comfortable stance, the batter has to feel ready and balanced in order to hit the ball with authority.

To see if he is ready, Coach Manju will usually test the first time batter in the following manner. For the first test he tells the batter to assume the batting position, and then, when the batter is ready, Coach pushes the bat from the top in a downward direction. Most batters will initially see their hands and bat drift down.

For the second test he tells the batter to hold the bat as tight as they can, and tests him in the same manner. Again the ballplayer usually will not be able to keep the bat up or hold his stance when coach pushes the bat down.

Before the third test Coach tells the ballplayer to totally relax. Then he tells him to hold the bat with firm wrists and stand balanced with their weight on the balls of the feet. Now when you push the top of the bat and apply pressure, the batter will be immovable and without tension. He is now in a ready and balanced position.

THE MECHANICS OF HITTING

THE LOWER EXTREMITIES

A. CRANK KNEE TO KNEE

As the pitcher winds up to throw the ball, the batter needs to "crank" or turn the front knee backwards toward the back knee. In Manju's baseball lingo, the "crank" is a starting or triggering, timing mechanism. This is similar to what others have termed "cocking" and/or "loading" the backside. The inward turning of the front knee closes the hip and sets the body to explode its power into the ball. Without the crank, the front side of the body "detaches" from the backside and there will be no power in the swing.

You have to time the pitch with your front leg.

A most important matter in cranking is to stay in balance. The batter's head should not be moving during the crank and the weight shift should be to the inside of the back foot and not to the outside. Coach Manju often has the batter tuck the front elbow in and back and this simple maneuver will facilitate a balanced position ready to explode on the next pitch. When cranking the total weight of the batter should be transferred to the inner half of the back leg. By bringing the front elbow in and back it is easier to stay in balance.

Tuck the Front Elbow in and Back

"Cranking" is also vital in throwing and pitching and will be touched upon in those chapters.

There are a number of ways to "crank." The Japanese ball players tend to raise the front leg completely off the ground as they start to crank.

For the slowly pitched ball, you can make a full crank by bringing the front knee all the way to the back knee. For a faster ball, a half-crank may be all the time you have. And for a very fast pitch, perhaps you have time only for an ankle crank or you may have to pre-crank. For the ankle-crank, think as though you're going to kick or flick a ball with your toes; kick and not push. You have to push off with the toes, not the heel. In the pre-crank, the batter is on his toes of his front foot with his left heel raised, and front knee is turned in awaiting the pitch.

Crank Knee to Knee

Types of Cranking:

1. Full Crank

   Front guide leg turns back into the direction of the back leg. We call this the "knee to knee" alignment. This movement allows the batter to crank or coil his hip before stepping forward in a straight line.

2. Half Crank

   Front guide leg turns back into the direction of the back leg but only half the distance, before stepping forward in a straight line. This is used when the pitch is faster.

3. Ankle Crank

   For an even faster pitch, the batter may only have time to quickly turn the ankle in and out and drive almost instantaneously.

4. Pre-Crank

   Front foot and ankle is turned in, with the weight on the balls of the foot, ready to pivot and step forward, before the pitcher throws the ball.

5. Mind Crank

   This is a difficult concept to write about. The batter has to instantaneously ready himself to hit the very fast ball coming his way by cranking in a fraction of a second. Coach Manju says he'll just say, "one-two" as fast as he can and his body is ready to drive and swing.

B. STEP OR STRIDE

Step

When the pitched ball is thrown, you simply step or stride forward with the front foot. However, the step has to be independent of the weight shift. It is important to delay the weight shift until you are ready to drive and swing in order to keep power in the bat. Shifting the weight to the front foot prematurely will weaken your swing. You have to step to the same place, the same spot, as you time the pitch with your front leg.

And refrain from pointing your toe at the pitcher because doing so will open your hip before the swing. When you keep the front foot closed, the hip will stay closed and allow you to hold back your power until you drive and swing. Dusty Baker, et al. suggests that the batter "pretend that he is stepping on thin ice" and that, "slow feet enhance fast hands."

If you don't pull with the left arm or if you don't step forward enough, you'll finish your swing with your body behind and the weight still on the rear foot. This is called a reverse drive (like a reverse pivot in the golf swing).

C. DRIVE

Then, as soon as the front foot touches the ground, pivot and drive with the right or back foot (for the right handed batter) towards the pitched ball. When you hit with the left (front) hand, the opposite action with the right (back) leg become very strong. On the other hand, if you swing with the right hand, you don't have the big action with the legs. Coach Manju tells them to squish the bug or smash the cigarette with the right foot. You're going to have lots of power because your swing is unobstructed. You push from the right foot, leg, hip and butt. The drive foot is also the clearance foot. You step, you drive and clear your hips, as you swing.

And Drive

When driving with the right leg, the right foot should turn toward the pitched ball. If the ball is on the inside, the front elbow leads and the driving foot turns in towards the ball. If on the outside, again the elbow leads and the driving foot turns less, but out towards the ball.

Through the Pitch

The sequence in batting is to "**crank, step, and drive**." You have to remember to follow this sequence. If the batter doesn't follow this sequence, for example if he swings before he steps and drives, that's when people will say that, "He's over-swinging," or "He's swinging too hard."

In many ways batting and throwing are similar and there is a truism in baseball, which goes, "The way you throw is the way you'll hit."

The position of your body after your swing should be where you started from. So if you lined yourself up with the front of the plate before you started, you should still be there after your swing. If you lunge at the ball or if you chop at the ball, you'll wind up in front.

Stay There

Don't Lunge

THE UPPER EXTREMITIES

FRONT ELBOW GOES TO THE BALL

From the ready and balanced launch position, the left or front elbow (in a right handed batter) goes to the ball, then your hands extend the bat until contact with the ball is made. You still use the right hand, but it follows the left elbow that guides the hands to the ball.

Front Elbow Goes to the Ball

SWING ON A DOWN-PLANE

The ideal swing is on a down-plane that is almost level. Since you start with the bat above your shoulders, if you pull the bat across the chest, you're going to have the proper down-plane.

Swing on a Down-Plane

SNAP THE BAT AT CONTACT

You start the swing by pulling the bat across the chest, and just before it comes in contact with the ball, the arms should be fully extended and your wrists should snap at the ball. That's when you hold the bat the tightest, right at contact. The hands should be parallel to each other and kept flat through the hitting area as you extend your arms.

Snap the Bat

PULL THE BAT UP

After contact, you pull the bat up over your left or front shoulder by bending (flexing) your elbows and swinging through to a high finish. The follow-through should bring your hands finishing up over your front shoulder. Don't roll your arms over because this will pull your body over and you will not be in a position to run towards first base.

Pull Bat Up After Contact

HIT THE BALL AS HARD AS YOU CAN BUT STAY BALANCED AND READY TO RUN

Remember Funai's mantra: "A bent spine cannot hit, a bent spine cannot throw."

Jensen Park: Family Collection.
Ready to run after hitting the ball

BATTING DRILLS

For most of the batting drills Coach Manju uses a large flexible net similar to a golf net. The coach crouches on one knee a few feet in front of and opposite the batter who is facing and hitting into the net. The ball is tossed with a

cadence to simulate a pitched ball. With this method each batter can have dozens of swings within a few minutes with the coach at his side.

Batting Drills, a Hundred Swings in a Few Minutes

ONE-HAND DRILL

At the start Coach Manju has the ballplayer take a wide stance, and without stepping, hit only with one hand (the front hand or left hand, in right-handed batters). He has the batter hold the bat up on the handle with only the left hand and practice just meeting the ball. If the bat is too heavy, the batter can support the fat part of the bat with his right hand. Or at home he can use a broomstick handle and using a wiffle ball and just swing, swing, swing. The left elbow has to go to the ball. The left arm hits the ball.

One-Hand Drill With Lead Arm

Two-hand Drill

Then, again without stepping, have the batter swing with both hands so there's a little more power, but it's the left that hits the ball. Concentrate on pulling the bat with the left arm.

Knee to Knee or Cranking Drills

Without a bat and with hands on hips, turn the front knee towards the back knee, and then step forward without shifting your weight. Remember, this is your timing mechanism. Learn how to time the pitch with your legs. Always step or stride to the same spot, directly at the pitcher without opening your hips.

Knee to Knee

Don't Open Your Hips

Driving Drills

Practice driving with the back leg. Feel as though you're squishing a bug with the balls of the back foot and push hard towards the pitched ball, using the power in the back of the leg. This is where the weight shift occurs. Remember, the power in hitting is in the legs.

CRANK, STEP AND DRIVE

Now the total weight comes in and pushes through from the back leg to the front. In summary, the sequence of hitting with the soft toss should be in this manner. Using a light bat we have the batter, without stepping, use the one or guide arm in hitting the ball. Next the two arm drill, without stepping. Next the two arms with the "crank, step and drive" sequence.

You can still add more power, by pulling harder with the left arm and driving harder with the right leg.

Crank

Step

Keep Front Hip Closed

Drive

Swing

and Follow Through

X-Drills

After the batter gets the mechanics of hitting, they can go into the X-drills. The "X" refers to the hitting zones: Up and out, up and in, down and out, down and in, and over the middle. The left elbow and right foot goes toward the ball. The soft toss is used by tossing the ball in an X-configuration in front of the batter. We toss the ball to position number 1 or low inside, number 2 or middle, number 3 or high outside, number 4 or low outside, number 5 or middle, and number 6 or high inside. The same X-drill is used for the soft toss at various speeds. Remember that for the inside pitch you have to swing quicker and further up the line than for the outside pitch where you have a fraction of a second more time.

Pepper Drills

These are an excellent way to practice total bat control, especially needed in a run and hit situation such as when a batter is asked to hit behind a base runner, or simply to advance a runner. Two to half a dozen players place themselves 15 to 20 feet or so in front of a batter who hits the thrown ball in sequence and in control to each fielder. Whoever fields the ball then throws to the batter whose aim is to hit the ball to each individual fielder.

Mind-Extension Drills

Mind extension drills can show how powerful the mind is. These drills help to develop a quicker bat swing and explosive contact on the ball. It is amazing how the mind can help to create more power, almost infinitely.

Once the batter starts to hit the ball squarely and consistently, coach tells them to imagine, to visualize, a second net behind the first one. The idea is to have the batter try to hit the ball harder, through the first net and into the second, by pulling harder and driving harder. As soon as the batter feels that he can hit through the first net, Coach then asks the batter to visualize a third imaginary net of the batter's favorite color or different color placed behind the second net, and so on, up to 20 nets, one net at a time. Coach does the soft toss and the batter hits one or several balls through each subsequent net. Any number of balls may be used per net depending on the batter's endurance. As he hits through the nets Coach constantly encourages the batter to create more mind power by pulling the guide arm elbow quicker to the ball or pivot the drive foot of the back leg faster toward the pitcher, or crank and step a little more forward to drive and transfer more power from the back leg to the front leg. Doing this in a systematic manner will result in a greater and harder impact on the ball into the net. Remember this is not a speed drill where we do the soft toss quicker or have the batter swing faster. We let the batter get into a ready position comfortably and firmly before each toss of the ball.

THE SEQUENCE OF HITTING WITH THE SOFT TOSS OVER THE MIDDLE OF THE HOME PLATE

1. Hitting in the free standing net number one.

2. Setting up an imaginary net of your favorite color a foot behind the first net and hitting through into the second net.

3. Then setting up imaginary net number three, four and so forth up to 20 nets.

4. The sequence of hitting with the soft toss should be in this manner over the middle of the home plate at various speeds – regular, faster, change-up. Up to 20 nets.

5. The sequence of hitting with the soft toss should be in this manner – inside, middle, outside of the plate with various speeds, regular, faster, change-up. 20 nets.

6. The sequence of hitting with the soft toss should be in this manner – the X-drills with various speeds, regular, faster, change-up.

MENTAL ASPECTS OF HITTING

The mental part of hitting is so very important. The good hitter studies the pitcher, what he throws under certain situations, what his strength and his weakness are, etc. The batter should show no fear of the pitcher and must be in a disciplined but aggressive state of mind.

An excellent retired professional ball player once said that by concentration and focusing he could often guess correctly what and where the pitcher was going to pitch next. He tried to put his mind in a state of total concentration so that he would not hear anybody or anything once the pitcher went into his wind-up.

QUESTIONS AND ANSWERS ON FAULTY SWINGS

1. WHAT CAUSES LUNGING WITH THE BAT?

This is a timing problem resulting in a faulty weight shift. The front foot is your "timing belt," your measuring stick. You have to step or stride forward but the weight has to be kept back until you are ready to drive. You have to keep your weight back even as you step forward, and as soon as the front foot touches the ground, then drive into the ball with your back leg as you swing. The weight shift will come with the drive.

Lunging

If you shift your weight forward together with the step or stride of the front foot, then the only thing you can do is to chop the ball into the ground because the spine is bent. You may hit the ball but you're only going to hit the ball into the ground.

2. A SOMEWHAT SIMILAR PROBLEM IS "OVER-SWINGING." ARE THEY THE SAME?

No. In "over-swinging" the batter seems to swing mightily but unsuccessfully at the ball. Coaches will often yell, "Don't swing so hard," or "Slow down your swing." However, the problem is not swinging too hard. The real problem is not following the proper sequence of batting which is crank, step, drive and swing. Instead the batter's sequence is crank, step, swing and drive. He is swinging a moment before his drive.

3. What causes the reverse drive or reverse pivot where the batter swings off his back foot?

This is a swing problem where the weight is not being shifted from the back to the front. Therefore he cannot reach the ball with the left or guide arm and there is no power to his swing. The solution to the problem is to take a longer step or stride with the front foot so that the weight moves forward as you drive into the ball.

Reverse Pivot

4. Swinging into a Pretzel

The batter who swings the bat right around his body often ends up twisted like a pretzel, sometimes finishing up by painfully striking his own back with the bat. The head may turn with the bat so his eyes are not on the ball. And the

legs are turned so he has trouble running to first base after he hits the ball. This may also lead to letting the back hand go off the bat or hitting one-handed because the shoulder may hurt in swinging around.

All the ills of the pretzel swing can be prevented by folding or flexing the elbows after striking the ball, thus pulling the bat over and around the front shoulder. Many people find it hard to understand this particular aspect of Coach Manju's concept of the full swing, but it is possible to swing hard without ending up like a pretzel, without turning your head and still be able to run toward first base with ease.

5. WHY DO SOME BATTERS HABITUALLY PULL THE BAT BACK AS THEY START TO SWING?

Usually that batter is triggering his swing with his hands. He holds his front elbow up and is timing the pitch with his hands instead of his front foot. The batter has to learn to time the pitches with his front leg and the path of the bat should be in a downward plane that is almost level.

Don't Pull Bat Back
Towards Catcher

And Drop the Bat

And Swing With an
Uppercut

6. WHY ARE SOME BATTERS CONSISTENTLY LATE WHEN FACING FAST BALL PITCHERS?

A common fault is the batter who has his back facing the pitcher in his set up or turns his back to the pitcher as the latter goes into his wind-up, in an effort to get more power into the bat. He also usually times the pitch with his hands. More often than not he's going to swing late because he has a long swing and his bat speed will seldom catch up to the ball.

Don't Turn Your Back
to the Pitcher

18

7. Why do some batters consistently hit the ball to the left (or to the right in left handed batters), pulling the ball foul more often than not, and out of play?

That's because his left arm is "locked" and the right turns and rolls over the left hand and arm. In addition his front hip is usually open. He may be quick with his hands but because he's locked, he pulls everything to the left. He may be able to hit the outside pitch but all other pitches will become foul balls because he's locked. The key to prevent locking is to tuck the front elbow in, then take the elbow to the pitched ball and swing with flat hands.

8. Manju, you teach the batters to always step forward to the same spot as the pitch is made. Then how is the batter going to hit the balls thrown to the inside and outside corners of the plate?

The front elbow has to go to the ball. For the inside pitch, you'll need a quicker, maximum pull with the left arm and maximum drive with the right or back leg to the inside. For the outside pitch, again the front elbow goes to the ball, and then you drive towards and through the ball with your right or back leg. The toes of the driving leg should point towards the pitch.

Bunting

Stance

There are two possible positions for the feet when preparing for the bunt. The old classic one is to bring the back foot up parallel with the front foot so that you are completely squared around and facing the pitcher. The second, and perhaps more recently favored one, is the one where the batter simply makes a half turn toward the pitcher without moving the feet. It is easier to cover the outer half of the plate with the bat with the older method, but it is easier to disguise the bunt a moment longer with the second. It is also easier to pull away from an inside pitch with the latter.

Standing at the very front of the batter's box makes it easier to keep the bunt in fair territory. It's best to hold the bat over and in front of the plate to assure that this occurs.

Classic Bunt Stance   Half Turn Bunt Stance

GRIP

The top hand slides up halfway on the bat, with the thumb and index finger cradling the bat near its trademark. The bottom hand assumes a light, relaxed grip, with the thumb, index and middle fingers and an open palm to cushion or deaden the pitched ball.

Keeping the head of the bat above the level of the handle will lessen the chances of a pop up.

Turn your shoulders to the right or left to place the bunt in the desired direction, towards first or third base, rather than directing the bat with your hands.

The Proper Way to Bunt   Not Like This

ELEVATOR APPROACH

Keep the distance, the relationship, between your eyes and hands constant. Your eyes should be just above and behind your left hand. Always start with the bat held at the top of the strike zone and avoid attempting to bunt any pitches above this level. Then for all lower pitches, lower your body by bending your knees, like coming down an elevator. Keeping the eyes to hand relationship constant or together will help to avoid any temptation to reach for or to poke or stab at the ball. Some coaches advise getting the feeling that you're catching the ball with your bat.

FAKING A BUNT

When faking a bunt the bat should be held in the path of the ball, then as the ball approaches the bat handle is pushed downward. This movement may impair the catcher's vision and timing and help your teammate who may be trying to steal a base.

TYPES OF BUNTS

1. SACRIFICE BUNTS

a. The object of the usual sacrifice bunt is to advance the base runner or runners. The batter should bunt the ball only if the pitch is a strike.

b. The ball should be bunted away from the infielders and pitcher, and as close to the baseline as possible, but in fair territory.

c. By holding the bat firmly but softly, and/or by bringing the bat backward on contact with the ball, you can "deaden" the bunt so that the ball will roll slowly.

2. SQUEEZE OR SUICIDE BUNT

The object of the squeeze or suicide bunt is to have the runner on third base score an important run. When given the signal to bunt, the batter cannot show his hand until the pitch is made and has to bunt the next pitch thrown because the runner will be breaking for home as soon as the pitcher goes into his wind-up.

3. SAFETY SQUEEZE

The only difference is that the runner will not be running through to home until the batter bunts the ball. The batter still has to attempt to bunt any ball, but if the bunt is not executed, the base runner should to be able to go back safely to third.

4. BUNTING FOR A BASE HIT

a. Fast Bunt or Drag Bunt
Just as the pitcher is about to release the ball take a small step back with the back foot (in order to see the movement of the pitched ball, to avoid getting hit by the pitch, and to be ready to run), slide your top hand half way up the barrel of the bat, and angle the bat so that ball is bunted towards the base line, preferably towards third base.

A fast bunt is even easier for the left-handed batter. He makes a quick pivot facing the pitcher, slides his left hand up the barrel of the bat, bunts and runs. He has a big advantage since he's two steps closer to first base to start with.

Take a Small Back Step With the Back Foot

Slide Your Right Hand Up

b. Push Bunt for a Base Hit

Bunt the ball past the pitcher towards the second baseman. On drag and push bunts you have to know how the defense is positioned since you are trying to get on base.

CHAPTER 2

THROWING

"I tell the parents, no "negatives" here. You can take all the pictures you like, but don't bring the negatives; no yelling, no screaming, no mad faces, no swearing. That's because I cry very easily and if I cry, you're in trouble. You'll have to leave, but your child can stay."

Everything in baseball comes back to throwing the ball correctly. One of the best high school coaches in Hawaii, Dunn Marumaru said, "The first thing I look for in a player is whether he can throw properly. If he can't throw, he can't play defense for me." He'll be a detriment on the field and may be limited to being a pinch-hitter, a pinch-runner and spend most of his time sitting on the bench.

If he can throw properly, the right-handed person can play any position in baseball. The left-hander, because of the nature of the game, may have to play at first-base or the outfield, or pitch.

Furthermore, pitching is throwing and throwing is pitching. The basic mechanics are the same. And if you follow the basic mechanics as taught by Coach Manju, you should be able to throw right at your target almost every time with practice, of course.

It has been said that the way you throw will usually be the way you hit. Coach Manju feels that the mechanics of throwing and hitting are essentially the same. So learn to throw properly and you'll hit properly.

This chapter is aimed at making the ball player throw correctly, accurately, and in a timely fashion. This often means that he has to get rid of the ball by throwing as quickly as possible in order to get a base runner out.

READY BALANCED POSITION

The ballplayer has to be in a ready and balanced position no matter what he's doing on the field. Whether he's getting ready to catch or throw the ball, or whether he is about to hit the ball, he has to be in a ready, balanced position.

Are You Ready?

Coach Manju has them assume a semi-crouched position with their knees and hips flexed, feet separated about shoulder width and weight on the balls of their feet. The right-handed player should have his left foot slightly in front of the right, and vice versa for the left-hander. Both hands are held up in front of him just below eye level with palms facing each other and elbows pointing down. The ballplayer in this position should be immovable, forward, backward or sideward. If Coach can push them over easily, they are not balanced. Once they are balanced and locked in, they are not going to be shoved off balance, and they can learn this feeling easily in a short period of time.

And Balanced?

Checking the coaches and/or ballplayers to see if they are in a ready balanced position is a mind opener. This often initiates awareness and is an awakening process because few individuals are consciously aware of whether they're balanced. But the individual has to be in a ready balanced position in order to perform any athletic act completely and well. Simply checking the individual to see if they're balanced will often make them sit and listen and ready to learn.

THREE BASIC TYPES OF THROWS

OVERHAND THROW

The head position should be straight up, leaning slightly back behind the front shoulder. The throwing arm should be up above the head, fully extended, with the front elbow pointing to the target. The back knee and the throwing arm should be in the same angle as the head position. Remember to pull the front hip around and backward as you throw so that the back leg can kick over the body, in total balance, with no stress or tension on the throwing arm.

Overhand Throw

THREE-QUARTER THROW

The "three-quarter throw" is a misnomer in that any throw made at an angle of between 10 to, perhaps 80 degrees, is called "three-quarter." The head should be tilted towards the throwing arm at an angle, with the hands up at eye level and the front elbow pointing to the target. The positions of the back knee and the throwing arm should be in the same angle as the head position. Remember to pull the hips around as you throw so that the back leg can kick over the body to the other side in total balance, with no stress or tension on the throwing arm.

Three-Quarter Throw

Side-Arm Throw

The head should be tilted at an angle approaching 90 degrees and the hands are near the ground, fully extended with an elbow to elbow movement. (Unlike other infield throws, the glove hand should be on the outside when making the elbow to elbow movement while cranking.) The guide arm should clear upward and the knee of the back leg should kick right through to the target, as the ball is thrown in balance. The side-arm throw should be taught when the ballplayer gets to be around 9 years old and can physically handle a baseball with ease. This is the age when the double-play becomes an important tool for the infielder.

Side Arm

In all three types of throws it is important to remember Coach Funai's mantra: ***The position of the head determines the action of the body which will follow.***

The ballplayer has to practice and learn all three types of throws because when quickness is necessary, he has to throw the ball from the position where he catches the ball.

For an infielder to throw out a very fast runner, he has to be able to release the ball from wherever and whatever position he fields the ball. Also, especially in attempting to make double plays, the infielder has to make a quick snap throw, often sidearm.

The Ills of Throwing

Front Side Problems

If the left or front side of your body is not working, you can still throw, but cannot throw with power.

a. The left or front foot has to crank and step at the target.

b. The left arm has to pull around the waistline. If the arm is extended at the elbow so that it is straight and/or pronated (turned down) you will lock yourself.

| Don't extend and lock left arm | Don't pronate left hand | Don't just drop the gloved hand |

c. On the other hand, if you simply drop the gloved hand to your side, or if you throw with your arms together, there will be no power to your throw. (Manju tells the kids, you'll look as though you forget your cup, because your hand comes down to protect your "dingdong" and they all laugh.)

Don't throw with your arms together

There'll be no power in your throw

BACK SIDE PROBLEMS

When the right or backside is not working, the weight will not transfer over and again there will be no power to your throw.

No Zip to Your Throw

a. It may look fancy and you can end up with a nice looking form, as though you are ready to have a picture taken, but there will be no zip to your ball.

b. You may end up kicking yourself in the okole (butt) with your back foot.

Backside Not Working

Results in a Kick in the Butt

c. Or you may wear out your right shoe as you drag it around rather than kicking forward with it.

LEADING WITH THE BALL

Leading with the ball will invariably lead to a weak or errant push rather than a strong throw. The ball should always be held facing down before it is thrown.

Never Lead With the Ball

THE MECHANICS OF THROWING

This is the sequence and mechanics of the basic five steps of throwing (for the right handed thrower). Learn them well and you'll never go wrong. Always start from the ready and balanced position.

STEP 1. STEP FORWARD AND PLANT THE RIGHT FOOT AT 90 DEGREES TO THE TARGET.

Plant Right Foot
90 Degrees

STEP 2. "CRANK" THE LEFT KNEE TOWARD THE RIGHT KNEE. AS NOTED IN THE PREVIOUS CHAPTER ON BATTING, CRANKING IS COACH MANJU'S TERM FOR GETTING THE BODY READY TO THROW (OR TO BAT).

Crank

STEP 3. STEP STRAIGHT FORWARD WITH THE LEFT FOOT AT THE TARGET.

Step to Target

STEP 4. PULL THE LEFT SIDE OF YOUR BODY, IN PARTICULAR YOUR ARM AND SHOULDER, DOWN AND AROUND THE WAIST.

Pull the Left Side

STEP 5. KICK WITH RIGHT LEG AS YOU THROW RIGHT AT THE TARGET.

Kick and Throw

POINTS OF EMPHASIS

The first step with the right foot should be in line with the target but the foot is planted at a 90 degree angle to the target.

"*Cranking*" the left knee toward the right knee turns the hip in. This shifts the player's weight to the right or back leg and torques the upper half of the body in preparation for the throw. If the throw has to be hurried, it can just be a half-crank, an ankle crank, or even a "mind-crank," but more about these later. The cranking has to be completed in order to make a powerful throw and to avoid straining your throwing arm.

The left is the guide arm. The left elbow has to come up and point to the target as your eyes look over the left shoulder at the same target. Then pull the guide arm down and around your waistline as your throw.

In pulling the left arm and shoulder down and around the waistline, the elbow cannot be in a completely straight or fully extended position. The left elbow has to be partially bent or flexed as it is pulled. (Try it. It's impossible to pull with the left elbow straight back in an extended position).

The left or front foot is the "*measuring stick.*" It should reach out and land just to the left of an imaginary line with the toes pointing at the target. If the foot lands to the right of the line you may "lock" yourself. As the left foot steps forward, the left knee should be almost straight, in an extended position, as the weight of the body is shifted forward.

The right or back leg is the power or kicking leg and drives the ball to the target. The kick will transfer the weight of the body from the right to the left side and over towards the target.

If you want to throw harder, just pull harder with the left arm and kick harder with the right leg.

Whether you go through the five steps of throwing very quickly or slowly, the throw will be just as accurate and strong. The important thing is that the sequence has to be followed.

THE CROW-HOP

"Crow-hop" is an old baseball term referring to the hop that a ballplayer makes as soon as he fields the ball and gets set to throw. Baseball is a game of inches and nano-seconds, so the quicker the ballplayer can get rid of the ball, the better his chances of making the play in time. He has to go through all the five basic steps of throwing, but in doing the crow-hop he abbreviates all the steps in his attempt to throw out the base runner.

So as soon as he fields the ball, he has to:

1. Hop forward toward the target and plant the right foot.

2. At almost the same moment, make a short crank and step forward with the left foot to the target.

3. Pull (the left side), kick (the back leg), and throw in rapid sequence.

After catching the ball you "crow hop" forward as high and close to the target as possible for the following reasons:

1. Hopping closer to the target will allow you to throw with more velocity and quickness just because you are closer to the target.

2. Hopping as high as you can will give you time so that your arms can get into position to throw before your legs land on the ground, ready to pull and kick.

3. It also allows you to clear all uneven surfaces from interfering with your throwing rhythm.

4. It allows your guide arm to center and align to the target before throwing.

5. Finally, because you crow-hop closer to the target, your throw will be at the best of control.

HANDLING THE BALL

The ball is held in the throwing hand with the thumb under and supporting the ball, and the index and middle fingers, held just slightly apart, on top of and on the seam of the ball. For the younger children, perhaps three fingers on top will be more comfortable and stable until they grow a little.

How firmly should the ball be held? Firm enough so that the ball doesn't fall out in the act of throwing. Coach Manju checks this by having the child hang on to ball with the correct grip as he tries to pull the ball away with two fingers. If coach can pull it out easily, the grip has to be firmed up but without any feeling of tension in the arm.

The palm of the hand and the ball should always be held facing down toward the ground before the ball is thrown. As soon as you pick up the ball keep it facing down towards the ground until you get into the throwing position. Otherwise you're going to be leading with the ball and it's going to fly over the target or into the ground when it is thrown.

Keep the Ball Facing Down

Coach Funai frequently used to say, **"elbow to elbow"**. The elbows should come together as the ball is brought into the throwing position, the gloved hand inside of the throwing hand, and then separated just before the throw is made. The right elbow pulls the ball up and back and the elbow leads and pulls the ball forward just before the wrist is snapped forward and the ball is let go. Just at the moment before the ball is released, just before the forward motion of the arm is made, the wrist is brought into the cocked position to **"break the tension in the wrist."** This is

35

Coach Manju's term for the cocking and subsequent uncorking of the wrist as the ball is released. The right elbow should be at least at a 90 degree angle for the ball to be thrown with power. If the angle formed by the forearm and the arm is less, you may be able to flip the ball but you will not be able to throw with much force.

For the short throw in the infield, the throw can be started with the ball at the height of your head. But when making the long throw from the outfield, you start with the ball all the way down, then reach as high as you can, then pull and kick hard as you throw.

All ball players have to learn to throw both short and long, so the infielder has to learn to throw like an outfielder and vice versa.

As the child gets older, and especially when he or she has to make the double play, they have to learn to throw from the three-quarter and side-arm positions. Remember Coach Funai's mantra: ***"The position of the head determines the action of the body."*** So, in making the three-quarter and side-arm throw, the head has to be tilted in the three-quarter or side-arm positions. The other principles are the same -- elbow to elbow, pull and kick, etc.

THROWING ON THE RUN

If you watch major league baseball on television you will often see infielders run in to field slow grounders and throw off their right foot in an attempt to throw the base runner out. No question that this type of throwing on the run has a place because it is required in beating a fast base runner. Throwing on the run will be required at the top level of baseball but is not advocated for younger players because it requires a strong, accurate and mature arm, lots of extra practice and a manicured ball field.

THROWING DRILLS

PULL AND TURN

From the basic balanced position, the left foot slightly in front of the right (for the right-handed player), hands in front and thumbs up, pull the left elbow back and around the waist several times on command.

Get Ready

Pull and Turn

CRANK AND STEP

From a position perpendicular to the target, crank the front or left knee (for right handed players) back and in toward the back or right knee ("knee to knee"), then step forward. The left foot should land with the toes pointing at the target.

Crank

And Step

ROCK AND KICK

Rock back, and then kick the right foot over towards the target to transfer your weight forward.

Rock   and   Kick

HIGH FIVE

A coach or parent stands a few feet in front with his hand held in front of him at shoulder height. The player then cranks, steps, kicks and slaps the coach's hand in a throwing motion. Subsequently, the coach steps back with his hand still held up, the player cranks, steps, kicks and goes through a hard throwing motion in front of and down with a complete follow-through motion. The front or left arm (in the right handed) is the guide arm, so raise the left elbow to the target, then straighten it so that the left hand and glove point right at the target.

THROWING FROM KNEELING POSITION

This a good drill for those who lead with the ball. From the kneeling position, learn how to throw by turning the hips. Emphasize elbow to elbow and the ball always facing down as it is brought up to be thrown.

THE SPLIT DRILL

A good drill for those who throw with both arms together. No ball is needed. Stand with your left foot slightly in front of your right and just pull the left side (for the right-handed player) around the waist and kick with the right leg as you make a throwing motion. Just doing this repeatedly, pull and kick, pull and kick a dozen to 15 times will warm you up and you'll be ready to throw a ball hard.

Crank

Step

Pull (your left side) and
Kick (your right leg)

INFIELDER'S DRILL OR ELBOW TO ELBOW

Leading with the elbows, with both arms up, the hands just above the head, bring them together, the gloved hand inside the throwing hand, and then pull them apart. The elbows should lead the hands and not vice versa. Keep doing this, elbows together, elbows apart, together, apart, elbows always leading the way.

Elbows Together

Then Start Elbows Apart

Elbows Apart

Then Throw

OUTFIELDER'S DRILL

Start with the ball all the way down, near the ground, and then bring the ball up leading with the elbows. The ball should be facing down as it is brought up, then reach as high as you can just before you release the ball.

Run and Catch	Crow Hop	Start Low	Then Reach as High as You Can

On occasion the outfielder has to make a "do or die," hurried catch and throw. On such an occasion, he has to field the ball on the glove side as he starts to crow-hop and reach as high as he can to make a strong, accurate throw.

"Do or Die"	Glove the ball	Crow Hop	Reach High

ALIGNMENT DRILLS (ZERO TO 360 DEGREES)

Alignment drills are absolutely necessary in order that the position player throws to the proper base or the correct cut-off person in order to nail the base runner. Every player needs to do these drills: the infielder, outfielder, catcher, and pitcher. Not infrequently, in the heat of battle, a teammate other than the player fielding the ball, will be better able to assess the situation and will yell at the player to throw to second instead of first base or vice versa. An outfielder, instead of trying to throw the base runner out at home plate, may be better off throwing to second base to prevent the batter from getting a free base. Decisions have to be made in a fraction of a second, at the spur of the moment, and thus the importance of the alignment drills.

1. Practice the alignment drills at 30, 90, 180, and 360 degrees.

2. "Bookends:" Momentarily bring your feet together, like bookends, before you step and throw. This is your "crank:" You have to crank, even though it may only be a half crank, an ankle crank or a mind crank, or else you will be stuck leading with the ball and unable to make a strong and accurate throw.

Ready   Bookends   Turn

3. Every time you turn and pivot, the right foot has to land first. The left has to step toward the target and, as soon as the left foot touches the ground, then pull, kick and throw. So the sequence is: bookends, turn, step and throw; bookends, turn, step and throw; bookends, turn, step and throw. Then do the alignment drills faster and faster with the crow-hop.

Step   and Throw

4. Practice the above alignment drills throwing overhand, three-quarter and side arm. However, for the 360 degree turn you should only throw overhand. The outfielders should always throw overhand for long throws to the bases or home plate in order to get a straight bounce off the ground, rather than chance a ricochet off at an angle with a side arm throw.

In summary, the first thing to be concerned is to be in total alignment. Stay in one spot and don't be jumping around. The second is, you have to re-crank your hands along with your legs, and how quickly you do this will determine whether you can beat the base runner. Thirdly, every time you turn and pivot, the right leg has to land first and the left has to step and throw.

SIDEARM DRILLS

1. Practice throwing sidearm with elbow to elbow movements and both hands near ground level. Clear the guide arm up and around and kick the back leg forward as you throw.

2. Drill with only the throwing arm at ground level.

3. Clapping the Hand Drills: Extend the guide arm with an open palm to the target, then kick and mimic a sidearm throw with an open hand and slap the fixed hand in a clapping motion.

"CHICKEN WING THROWS"

These drills are called "Chicken Wing Throws" because the fielder's elbows are positioned and move like chicken wings.

1. "No -step Chicken": When having to make a short throw to execute a double play or quick force out, the primary fielder pivots towards the base and flips or tosses the ball without stepping. The fielder has to keep the ball in front of his body so that it is always visible to the receiver. Anytime the receiver loses sight of the ball it will become difficult for him to catch it since he is so close to the primary fielder

2. "One-step Chicken": Again, when throwing from a short distance, the primary fielder pivots and takes a quick short step towards the base and flips sidearm to the secondary fielder.

3. "Crow-hop Chicken": Upon fielding a grounder or line drive, the fielder crow-hops and throws sidearm to make a longer throw.

THE UNDERHAND TOSS AND BACK FLIP

These are both short throws, primarily by infielders. The advantages of these throwing methods are that they are time saving and the ball is always visible to the person who is catching the thrown ball.

Back Flip From Shortstop to Second

CHAPTER 3

PITCHING

Make the child happy and teach them with smiles. We joke a lot with the kids and their parents. We tell them smile, because you're not in prison. And when the child does something good, we tell them, "That's it, you're getting there, you're really getting there."

Although not every youngster can become a pitcher, anyone can learn how to pitch by learning the essentials of throwing a baseball properly. Certainly it helps to have a strong arm, but any youngster who is willing and able can learn to pitch effectively.

In addition to having a strong arm, the most important ingredient to success is control and it is here that Coach Manju feels he can help the most. The keys to control are complete balance and total alignment. With his system of balance and alignment, and practice, of course, Coach feels that the pitcher should be able to throw a strike practically every time he throws. Warren Spahn, the great major league southpaw for the Braves, once proved that he could throw strikes repeatedly with his eyes closed, and perhaps all pitchers should feel the same way.

Control is not only throwing strikes, but being able to throw the ball where you want to throw it, and not infrequently, outside of the strike zone.

The pitcher, probably more than any other player, plays a pivotal role in a baseball game. Keeping the opposition batters off the bases and from scoring is half the game. The good pitcher can control the game by skillfully adjusting the speed and location of his pitches to keep the batter off balance, and that is the name of the game.

Pitchers should always try to throw a first-pitch strike. It's much easier to stay ahead in the count that way. Certainly, at least the second ball should be a strike. Otherwise you're starting behind and the batter has a great advantage.

PITCHING FROM A FULL WIND-UP

THE STANCE IN READY AND BALANCED POSITION

There are many different pitching forms but the fundamentals and mechanics of pitching are the same. The pitcher should be relaxed and comfortable whether throwing with a full wind up or from a stretched position. Stand with your feet slightly and comfortably apart on the rubber. There may be an advantage to standing on the right corner of the rubber for the right-handed pitcher, in order to catch the opposite corner of the home plate.

THE WIND-UP AND ALIGNMENT

1. First take a small step back with your left foot (for the right handed pitcher) just off the rubber, keeping your head aligned to your target.

2. Then step, turn and secure the right foot against and parallel to the rubber. This is akin to a sprinter securing his back foot with the starting block in a track meet.

3. Crank knee to knee into a balanced position. Manju calls this the third position balance. It has also been called the "*tuck*" or the "*crane position*."

    The concept of "*toe-to-toe*" has to be kept in mind in order to prevent the hips from opening up too quickly and to keep the pitches down in the strike zone. During the pitcher's crank, the front foot (including toes) should be pointing downward and kept facing down as he steps forward and finally points forward at the target. His weight should be totally on his backside in a balanced position.

Step, Pull and Kick

Keep in total alignment by stepping with your lead foot right at the target. The foot should land just to the left (for the right hander) of a straight line to the target.

To throw a fastball the pitcher should step as far as possible towards home plate. The opposing but synchronous movement of pulling the left side and kicking the right side over will help to increase the velocity of your pitches.

To throw other pitches such as a curve ball, the guide leg should extend and step a shorter distance in order to allow the hips to reverse inward and backward and to allow the throwing arm to snap down or to the side for maximal movement of the ball. The movement of the ball is controlled by the pitcher's grip and wrist action.

Release

During the wind-up, start with the ball down and behind you, and then reach as high as you can, like the outfielder's throw. As the hands separate to initiate the throw, the elbow of the guide arm should point up and then to the target while the elbow of the throwing arm should be pointing and pushing downward; the hand and ball should be facing and reaching toward the ground. Then from here, leading with your elbow, reach up and throw as you pull and turn.

No matter what the rhythm, the pitcher should reach up and pitch from a high release point to make the ball travel on the downward plane. Pitching Coach Bob Shaw feels that the key to pitching success is the ability to throw the ball on a downward plane.

Pitch From the Same Release Point

Whether pitching a fastball, curve or slider the position of the arm and hand should be kept constant and the ball released from the same point. This helps to develop control and also helps to avoid tipping your pitch off to the batter.

THE FOLLOW-THROUGH

The pitcher's arm travels forward, down and across his body and points toward the opposite ankle as he completes his pitch. Then almost immediately, he has to reverse back and resume the ready balanced position for the possibility of fielding a ball batted back to him.

CHANGING THE RHYTHM AND SPEED OF A PITCH

As noted in the section on throwing, one has to learn to crank in order to throw properly. In pitching, one generally utilizes a full knee-to-knee crank for most pitches, but he can become just as effective with a half-crank or a minimal ankle crank with practice. The smart pitcher can utilize this change in rhythm to keep the batter mentally off stride, by going slow, faster or really fast.

THE FIGURE EIGHT CONFIGURATION AND RHYTHM

The path of the ball starting with the wind-up and proceeding to the point of release outlines an abbreviated figure eight configuration. The rhythm that outlines this configuration allows the component parts of the arm to become ready to throw strongly and accurately.

By following the above principles of pitching one should be able to throw strikes with ease and, with practice, even with your eyes closed.

PITCHING FROM THE STRETCH OR SET POSITION

With runners on the bases one has to pitch from the stretch or set position. Baseball is a game requiring speed and quickness and nano-seconds often times determines the difference between being safe or out, between a run being scored or not. And it's largely the pitcher's job to prevent the base runner from stealing bases.

FEET POSITIONS

The pitcher's right (of front) foot is parallel to and just touching the rubber. The left (or front) foot should be in front of and parallel to the right (or back) foot. It may be positioned a few inches towards third-base but not towards first.

HAND POSITIONS

The hands are initially separated and stretched up, then brought down to the set position at head, face or waist levels before throwing to the batter. By bringing both hands up over the head, as the pitcher slowly brings his still separated hands downward he can stop at any point to pivot and attempt a pickoff play. By varying the speed of the up and down motions getting into the set position, the smart pitcher can have the base runner at his mercy. Once he gets into the set position the pitcher's guide arm should be tucked against his body as he looks back and forth between the bases and home plate.

HEAD POSITION

The head should be held straight up as he looks over his shoulder. In this position it is easy to turn and look towards the bases. When the head is flexed or bent down on his chest, the pitcher is limited in looking to first-base and will put a strain on your neck.

The pickoff throw by the pitcher should be an overhand throw if initiated while the hands are still in the area of his head, a three-quarter throw if initiated with the hands in the area of his face or shoulders, or a side-arm throw if down at the waist.

THE SLIDE-STEP

The slide-step was devised so that the base runner would have a harder time stealing a base off the pitcher's wind-up. However, you can easily hurt your pitching arm if you simply slide your forward foot without some sort of a crank. You cannot go forward without your arm getting up in the throwing position.

The solution is to make a quick ankle crank that will bring your front hip in before you step and throw. Just a quick kick of the ankle, a toe to toe maneuver, will give your arm the moment necessary to get into position. In essence, you kick your front foot into balance to get your mechanics back into rhythm.

THE PICKOFF

The pitcher's primary concern with men on bases is to hold the runners on the bases. It's fine to be able to pick off the base runner but that should not be the prime concern.

When throwing to the bases, the right-handed pitcher has to pivot and shift his weight on his right foot, then turn on his left foot as he throws in order to have power and velocity to his throws. The right foot has to land first, the left has to step and throw.

The smart base runner often tries to time the pitcher's intervals as he schemes to steal a base. Therefore, the pitcher should alter the time it takes to reach his stretch position as well as the intervals of his pitches from the stretch position so as to disrupt the runner's timing. Altering the crank with his usual or regular motion is another way the pitcher has to keep the base runner guessing.

Pickoff plays have to be practiced with the catcher and all the infielders. More than one type of pickoff should be practiced to every base.

It behooves the pitcher to step off the mound after taking a stance, or make a throw to a base to see if the batter may inadvertently tip off his intention to bunt.

TIMING THE PICKOFF THROW

Once the base runner has achieved his lead and leaning back toward the base, it is very difficult to pick him off. The best time to pickoff a runner is when the runner is leaning or stepping away from the base to get his lead.

1. If the runner tends to hop off the base, the pitcher should throw as soon as the runner starts his hop.

2. If the runner stretches out his lead by sliding his feet a half step at a time, the pitcher should throw as soon as he starts his slide.

3. If the runner uses a cross-over step to stretch his lead, the pitcher should throw as soon as the back step begins.

4. If the pitcher looks back at the base coach, the pitcher should throw as soon as the runner turns his head away from the pitcher.

The left-handed pitcher has an advantage for the pickoff when a base runner is on first base because he is facing directly at the runner. The pitcher can freeze the runner by bringing his front leg up with the knee and hip in a cranked position and can throw to either first base or to the batter as long as the front leg does not go behind and beyond the pitcher's plate.

TYPES OF PICKOFF SIGNALS

1. Counting system between the pitcher and infielder, e.g. 1, 2, and 3, or 1001, 1002, 1003.

2. "Daylight" system where the pickoff throw is made as soon as the pitcher sees the infielder between the base and base runner.

3. Head, hand or leg signals between the pitcher and infielders.

4. Verbal signals or whistling between pitcher and infielders.

PICKOFF PLAYS TO SPECIFIC BASES

A. PICKOFF PLAY AT FIRST BASE WITH RUNNERS ON FIRST AND SECOND

1. When the pickoff signal is activated by the first baseman, he moves away from the base and the pitcher initially looks towards second base. Then as soon as he looks towards home plate, the first baseman moves back to the base, the pitcher pivots and throws to him.

2. When the pickoff play is activated by the catcher, the pitcher looks towards second base longer than usual.   Then when the catcher drops his glove the first baseman breaks for the base, the pitcher pivots and throws for the pickoff.

B. PICKOFF PLAY AT SECOND BASE

1. When the shortstop is receiving the pickoff, the second baseman initially moves towards the base, and then decoys the runner by moving away from the base. When the runner takes a bigger lead, the pickoff throw is made to the shortstop.

2. Similarly, the shortstop can decoy the runner, allowing the pickoff play to the second baseman.

3. When the shortstop or second baseman signals the catcher for a pickoff, the catcher relays the signal to the pitcher. The pitcher must not look at second base. As soon as the catcher sees the shortstop or second baseman break for the base, he drops his glove, signaling the pitcher to pivot and throw to second.

4. In the swing move with a runner on second base, the pitcher lifts his leg to begin his delivery but instead of striding toward the plate, he swings his leg toward second base while keeping his eyes toward home.

5. The fake wheel play. When the batter is trying to bunt the runner on second base to third, the shortstop comes off the bag in front of the runner and breaks toward third base as though the wheel play was in effect. If the batter follows, the pitcher turns and throws to the second-baseman.

C. PICKOFF PLAY AT THIRD BASE

1. When the pick-off signal has been activated, the third baseman decoys the runner by moving away from the base. When the pitcher from the set position slowly lifts his front leg, the third baseman breaks for the base for the pickoff.

2. If the runner takes a good-sized lead before the pitcher gets set and before his wind-up, a moment before the pitcher winds up, the

catcher will drop his glove signaling the pitcher to pivot and pickoff the runner.

D. PICKOFF PLAY AT FIRST BASE WITH RUNNERS AT THE CORNERS

From the stretch position, the pitcher fakes a throw to third, pivots and throws to first base if the runner has left the base.

E. PICKOFF PLAYS WITH THE BASES FULL

When the bases are full of runners the primary concern is the front runner who can score. Not infrequently the back end runners take a huge lead since the focus is often not on them and it is easier to pick a runner off first or second base in that situation.

CHAPTER 4

FIELDING

Stan told me, "You can never change the kid. The kid's got to change himself." The kid has to feel what you're talking about. You don't make the boy good. The boy makes himself good.

In fielding a ball, you first have to be in a ready and balanced position. Your legs are spread apart with the left foot (for the right-handed player) slightly in front of the right. You open both knees, crouch comfortably with a straight back and weight on the balls of the feet. Your elbows are down and your hands up and facing each other in front of your chest, not too close, not too far, ready to reach out to field the ball. If you're totally balanced, you can stay in this position all day, yet you're ready to run and react in any direction.

Testing should be done exactly as in the ready and balanced position for throwing. In the beginning the ballplayer may not be able to achieve an immovable stance because his mind

Ready and Balanced

will be totally on the tester. The ballplayer's concentration and focus should be on the baseball coming into the glove so that he fields the ball cleanly.

From here, as the ball comes towards you, lead with the elbows and open your hands to catch the ball. When you lead with your elbows you'll find that you will be quicker turning to the ball. Try to catch everything in front of your body and not too close to your body if possible.

If the ball is up, you bring the elbows and hands up. If the ball is higher, jump first and bring the elbows up. If the ball is down, you open (spread) your knees, "shovel" your hands forward and field the ball as it comes into the glove. Watch the ball come into your glove.

The position of the hands and glove is very important. In general, if the ball to be fielded comes at you above your waistline, your hands and glove have to be up. However, if the ball comes at you below your knees, the hands and glove have to be turned down and open.

FORM FIELDING

The three elements of form fielding for grounders are "run, break down and center."

As soon as the ball is batted, you run as fast as you can towards the ball. We have the ball players run while holding the last three fingers of his hands clenched with the thumbs pointing up, and moving his arms up and down with bent elbows, as though he is pulling down on a rope.

Just before you get to the ball, you have to "break down," a term that in totality means getting into the ideal fielding position by taking shorter or shuffle steps just as you approach the ball, crouching down to a lower level and timing the ball. It means watching the bounce of the ball and getting ready to field the ball. Timing,

Run to Ball

coordination, rhythm are some of the words used to explain what breaking down means. At the moment just before fielding the ball, the ball player has to slow down, get into position and be ready to field the ball.

Break Down

And finally, you "center" by placing the feet down, the right foot first (for right handers), then the left, with toes pointed straight ahead, so that the ball is right in front and in the middle, in the very center, of your stance. We bend our body and knees forward and with both hands, we shovel forward to field the ball. The glove hand stays on the bottom, reaching for the ball, and the throwing hand above to grab and pull the ball out of the glove.

Center

At this moment, you should feel completely balanced and focused on reaching for and watching the ball come into your glove. Then crow-hop forward to your target and throw.

THREE TYPES OF GROUND BALLS

1. **Regular, Evenly Bounding Grounder:** Although it may be coming at the fielder very quickly, this is the easiest ball to field.

2. **High Grounder:** To field a high bouncing ball the fielder must follow the movement of the ball and try to catch it at or near the peak of the bounce. Otherwise he should try to field it on the short hop as it bounces upward again. The in-between hop is the most difficult ball to field.

3. **Grounder Spinning Out of Control:** Sometimes when the ball is struck near the top of the bat, the ball may spin more than it bounces in a crazy erratic manner. The fielder must run at full speed to get to the ball because it does not get to him as fast as the usual grounder, and he must field the ball with his glove and not the bare hand because it will be moving erratically and can easily spin out.

FIELDING DRILLS

*Note: Paper balls are used for all the drills when dealing with youngsters who are new to the game. The paper balls are made by crumpling two full sheets of newspaper into the shape of a round baseball. We then use elastic "pre-wrap" to cover the paper. Finally, we finish by completely wrapping the ball with athletic tape. The balls can be made to the approximate size of a baseball or softball by adding or subtracting sheets of newspaper.

RUN, BREAK DOWN, AND CENTER DRILLS

Coach Manju drills them in form fielding by making the fielders go up and down the field, without the ball, and on command to "Run," "Breakdown," and "Center," first in slow motion, then faster and faster.

In running, the upper extremities are almost as important as the legs. The thumbs of both hands should be pointed up to the sky, and then you pull the elbows down and back, close to your body, for maximum thrust with each stride.

Everyone's break down point varies. The bigger and slower players generally have to break down earlier. It is a matter of timing, coordination and rhythm as you get set to field the ball coming to you.

Center and Shovel

And in centering, the right-hander plants his right foot first, and then his left, with toes pointed straight ahead, in a wide comfortable stance with the ball in the middle of this stance. The larger the spacing or opening between the legs, the easier it will be to feel balanced and focused as you reach for the ball. You shovel your hands forward, the gloved hand on the bottom to receive the ball and the throwing hand ready to take it out of the glove to throw. When fielding grounders coaches have always been saying, "Don't let the ball play you." The fielder has to determine where he should be picking the ball up, although this is not always possible.

MOVEMENTS OF THE HANDS

From a ready and balanced position the ball player's hands are held in front of his chest, facing each other. Just before catching the ball, the palms are opened with the fingers separated evenly and in a cupped position. We move our elbows to the left or right in the direction of the ball. If the ball is up, both hands are raised up before catching the ball. If the ball is down, both hands are shoveled forward and our knees are opened so that we can bend lower to the ground just before we secure the ball with our hands. If possible you should attempt to field the ball in front of your body rather than to either side. Also, if possible, you should see the ball go into the glove, because if you don't, the ball may drop out of the glove because you were not able to squeeze and secure the catch.

To absorb the shock or impact of a hard hit or thrown ball, we should give way backwards just a bit as we catch the ball. If we open our palms without giving way to the hard hit ball, we may suffer bone bruises of the hands.

MOVEMENTS OF THE FEET

From a balanced, ready position, if the ball comes to our left, we hop to the left side with the right foot taking a back step behind the left. If the ball comes to our right, we hop to the right with the left foot stepping in front of the right.

Ready and Balanced Position

Jump and Reach With Your Hand

Open Your Knees and Shovel Forward

We move in balance and quickly with our glove ready to catch the ball by leading with our elbows to the left or right. To catch a ball that is going above our head, we position ourselves in a ready form, crouching so the legs can be used as spring to jump upward for maximum extension. As we jump, both hands go up and the glove hand is extended further to reach out for the catch. Remember to make an attempt to catch everything in front of your body.

To catch a low ball below our knees, we position ourselves in a balanced, ready form, crouched near ground level in order to see and to get in rhythm with the bouncing ball. Our legs and knees should be opened wide to allow us to get further down before shoveling our hands to receive the ball.

REACTION DRILLS

1. The fielders are told to go to the right or go to the left on command, using the back step. The ball is thrown to the right, then to the left, or up or down, and the fielder is told to try catching everything in front of them.

2. For a soft fly, the ball is caught by opening the hands like a flower.

3. For a hard hit liner or hard throw, the fielder is taught to pull back the legs to absorb the shock as the ball hits the glove.

4. Pivot and Turn: 360 degrees one way, and reverse, leading with the elbows

5. Pepper Drills for throwing and hitting.

6. For youngsters new to the game, drills can be done indoors or outdoors using paper balls and plastic bats.

LEFT AND RIGHT CLEARANCE DRILLS

Balls that fall in between the fielders and are not caught are called base hits. But if any of these balls are caught, then it's an out and could stop a rally or turn the outcome of a game. It's not unusual to see players field a ball hit to his right or left, quickly and beautifully, but be unable to throw the runner out. The ball is caught but the fielder is running in a direction from which he cannot readily get himself into a position to throw the runner out. These exercise drills will help a ballplayer to move to the left or right as fast as possible and quickly get into a position to make an out, or to field the ball and throw out a runner. He needs to learn and practice the left and right clearance drills until they become automatic.

THE LEFT CLEARANCE DRILL

When the ball is hit to the left side, we pivot, turn and run at maximum speed toward the approaching ball. With the glove hand in a ready position at knee level, we field the ball. Then we pull the glove hand up and pivot our body toward the receiver with a crow hop by bringing the right leg around and behind the left leg and securing a toehold. This allows the fielder to push off and throw with velocity toward the receiver. Again, on balls hit to the left side, as soon as you catch the ball, you have to hop into position. As soon as the ball is fielded, you hop and plant your right foot behind the left foot, then make a strong step to the target with the left foot and throw. (If the ball is caught behind you, then you may have to do a 360 degree turn, but that will come later.) If this movement is not executed you will be fielding the ball and, running at full speed and be unable to turn. Even if the ball is caught we would have to throw at a 90 degree angle toward the receiver without having any zip to the throw.

Run Left and Catch the Ball

Start Crow Hop

Crow Hop and Throw

Field the Ball

Get Ready to Crow Hop

Throw

THE RIGHT CLEARANCE DRILL

On balls hit to the right side of the fielder, we pivot, turn and run at full speed to the ball. The glove is opened as wide as possible with fingers pointed downwards. With the elbow leading the way, we scoop or may need to backhand the ball into the glove. As soon as the ball is fielded, we get into a throwing position taking the biggest step possible with the right leg in order to brace our body from running further, then we push off, throwing the ball as quickly as possible toward the receiver. Again, as soon as you field the ball, you have to plant the right foot, "rock," and throw. The term "rock" means to rear back and crank. Then you drive forward and throw hard.

A quick release of the ball is the key to getting the runner out.

May Need to Backhand   Plant the Right Foot   "Rock" and Throw
the Ball

Double Play Positions

Second Baseman Positions

The second baseman has four types of double play positions:

1. You can straddle the base, then depending on where the throw is coming from, step right or left to catch the ball, crow-hop and throw to first base.

2. You can position yourself behind the base awaiting the ball, and as soon as you receive the ball, touch the base with your left foot, push off as you take a back step away from the base runner and throw.

| Touch the Base With Left Foot | Back Step | Rock | and Throw |

3. If your teammate gets the ball before you arrive at second base, signal him by showing your glove as a target, step over the base and away from the runner as you catch the ball, slide the back foot across the base, crow-hop toward first base and throw.

Show Your Glove   Slide Back Foot   and Throw
                         Across Base

4. If you are late getting to the base, try to stay in line with the base and your teammate so that he has an easy target to throw to. As soon as you catch the ball, step on the inside of the base with your left foot, pivot and throw.

Stay In Line   With Base and   Catch   and Throw
                  Teammate

Always step towards first base in making the throw. Don't step backward towards left field because invariably the throw will not have a zip to it and will arrive too late to complete the double play.

SHORTSTOP POSITIONS

The shortstop has three types of double play positions:

1. When the first baseman or pitcher starts the double play from the confines of the infield, the shortstop should go inside of the base-path, to present an easy target to throw to, away from the runner. Then he can pivot and throw.

Go to the Inside of Base-path

2. On the other hand, if the second baseman, and sometimes the first baseman, starts the play outside the confines of the infield, the shortstop should usually go outside of the base and base-path to field the throw.

Stay Outside

3. If the shortstop is late getting to the base, he has to get in line with the base and the thrower to give the latter an easy target to throw to.

Get in Line   With Base and Thrower   Before Reaching the Base

OUTFIELD DRILLS

LINE DRIVES

Always be in a ready, balanced position with both hands facing each other and held in front of your chest, right below the chin. When catching the ball the palms of both hands are held open with the fingers separated evenly in a cupped position. If there is a line drive coming at you around your waist and chest, lower both knees with the hand position still below the chin. If you don't lower your knees the palms of both hands will automatically turn up, and the ball may hit the edge of the glove and skip upward and hit your face. If the line drive comes at you around or below the knees, then the glove should face downward, ready to be shoveled forward to receive the ball.

FLY BALLS

From a balanced, ready position with both hands facing each other, when the fly ball is about to be caught, both hands must open into a position like an open flower. The fingers are opened to prevent the ball from hitting and injuring the fingers.

When catching the ball above your head, your hands and arms may obstruct the view of the ball and cause you to lose your balance. In catching the ball below your chin unless you watch the ball go into your glove, it is not difficult to misjudge the ball. To absorb the shock of a ball from a high height, bend both elbows from the flower position.

LEFT POSITION AND RIGHT POSITION RUNNING

From the balanced, ready position and facing home plate, the ball player has to run as fast as possible towards the ball as soon as it is struck. At the same time an effort should be made to prevent your head from bobbing up and down by running on the balls of your feet. As you approach the ball, you must breakdown and pivot on your left leg if the fly ball is going over the left side of the body, or breakdown and pivot on your right leg if the fly ball is going over the right side of the body. You then reverse your feet as you make the catch, crow hop and throw to the cut-off man as fast as possible.

CENTERFIELD POSITION RUNNING

From the ready balanced position, when the fly ball or line drive is hit directly over you, pivot either to the left or right. You should be looking at the ball with your head up. Maximum effort should be made in running for the ball on the balls of the feet. If the ball moves to the right or left side when you are running, then pivot to that side to keep the ball in sight. As the ball comes down, you must breakdown, reverse your feet as you make the catch, crow hop and throw the ball to the cut off or relay person.

OVER THE SHOULDER CATCH

This is a situation where the fly ball is directly over the fielder's head and there is no time to turn around and reverse the body to get under the ball for the catch. The fielder's only chance is to run at maximum speed and look for the ball over his head. Both hands should be stretched out as far as possible above the head to cradle the catch to your body.

The drills for the over the shoulder cradle catch should have four different running directions. The feeder's (coaches') position should be in one place and the fielders should be in four separate lines, about 10 to 20 feet away from the feeder. Two lines should be in front of him, one to the left and one to the right. Two lines should be behind him, one to the left and one to the right. All fielders should run individually passing him, left first, and then rotate to the right. The feeder tosses the ball over their shoulders as they turn to look over the shoulders for the ball. After the two lines of receivers have passed him, the feeder then turns around and faces the other two lines and begins the drill all over again.

In a subsequent drill, the outfielders can throw to the bases to pick off runners after catching the ball.

TAGGING THE BASE RUNNER

Whenever a fielder tags a base runner around his head, body or upper part of his legs, more often than not the tag is too late and the runner is safe. It is best to tag the runner's foot or hand as he reaches for the base.

Whenever possible the fielder should be straddling the base in a crouched position, waiting for the ball. From this position he should be able to catch any ball coming his way, then quickly position his glove in front of the base, waiting for the sliding base runner. Even if the runner slides away from the base, the fielder can quickly cover the edges of the base to tag the runner's hand or foot.

If the runner decides to run through the base and you, you can quickly step forward, tag him and spin away at the same time, to avoid a collision injury.

CHAPTER 5

BASE STEALING AND SLIDING

BASE STEALING

Most bases are stolen off the pitcher rather than the catcher so it is most important for the base runner to study the pitcher's motions carefully. Certainly it helps to have quickness and speed, but one also has to know when to steal a base.

Some pitchers have different motions when they throw to the plate as opposed to when they throw to first base and they are easy to steal off. However, the wily pitcher will try to make the initial motions similar. If the right-handed pitcher lifts his left heel first he is throwing to the batter but if he lifts his right heel first, he is throwing to first. Some right-handed pitchers will keep their chin tucked under his left shoulder as he peers toward the runner on first base, and has to bob his head up when he throws to the plate so this is a good tip to steal. When throwing to the plate he has to keep his shoulder and hip "closed" so this is also a good time to steal.

It is harder to steal off a left-handed pitcher because he is looking directly at you on first base. The wily pitcher will be looking at his catcher while bringing his leg up and throw you out. However, sometimes the southpaw pitcher will have a higher leg kick when throwing to the plate, or show the bottom of his shoe when throwing home and the base stealer can go when he sees this. If his toe is pointed down, he is going to throw to first. Or he may have to close his front shoulder further when throwing to first.

Remember, if the pitcher, left- or right-handed, swings his front foot past the back edge of the rubber as he cranks, he has to throw to the batter. If he throws to the base runner at first, this is a balk.

At any rate, if you've got the steal signal from your coach, take a good lead, make your first step a crossover step, keep your head down and run.

SLIDING

Sliding to the bases and avoiding the fielder's tag requires practice and skill. Sliding can be dangerous, especially for the beginner, so it is important to learn this skill. In this section Manju will teach the basics of sliding feet first.

Sliding head first is not advocated and will not be taught because it is fraught with danger to head, neck and hands and you cannot reach the base any faster by doing so. However, the head first slide may be necessary when sliding back to the base on a pick off play. Furthermore, you'll see the head first slide in the professional, college and high school levels of play.

For initial practice sessions, have the ball players remove shoes and spikes, and wear sliding pads or shorts under long trousers or baseball pants. The practice grounds should be well sodded, and/or covered with large cardboard panels or large plastic sheets with running water. Or you can practice on a sandy beach as the waves recede back to the sea.

THE BASICS

1. While running to the base and just before sliding, get as low as possible to avoid injury from pounding into the base path from too high a position.
2. Depending on the position of the fielder and position of his glove, the runner can slide to either side to avoid the tag, touching the base with his extended foot or with his hand. If the fielder has not yet caught the ball, the runner can slide into the fielder and/or his glove to block the throw.

3. Don't change your mind once you've decided to slide. Go through with the slide even though there is no play on you to avoid injuring yourself by trying to stop suddenly.

THE STRAIGHT-IN SLIDE

This slide is the fastest way to get to the next base. You slide straight forward on your buttock with the top foot and leg extended and the bottom leg tucked under and behind the top leg.

SLIDING DRILLS, IN SEQUENCE

1. Practice starting the slide by crouching with your left hand touching the ground, then leap forward into the sliding position by turning to land on the left buttock and thigh.

2. While lying on the ground in the sliding position on your left side, spread your legs apart then bring them together, pretending that your legs are a pair of scissors cutting the grass. You slide on your left side so that you're ready to proceed to the next base.

3. Then, lying on your back, but turned on the left side with the left foot tucked under the right leg, reach for the base with your right foot.

THE POP-UP SLIDE

Whenever there is a chance for the runner to take an extra base, perhaps because the fielder missed the throw or the ball is deflected away, the runner can use the "pop-up" slide. It is like the straight-in slide except that it is started closer to the base and both legs are bent at the knees. As soon as the foot touches the base, the runner leans forward and, pushing up on his knees and jumping up on his feet, he can be off and running to the next base.

CHAPTER 6

MANJU'S TEACHING PHILOSOPHIES

EVERYTHING IS DONE BY THE KID'S FEELINGS.

You gotta make the kid taste it, taste how good it is. You can tell the kid that this is the way to throw a ball or hit a ball, but in order to really get it, he has to feel it. He has to feel how good it is to throw the ball right or hit the ball solidly. And when the kid starts throwing harder, hitting harder, he's going to change because he likes it and wants to keep that feeling.

I TELL PARENTS AND COACHES, DON'T GO GRABBING THE KIDS TOO MUCH.

Let them do it on their own because they're going to correct themselves. Just encourage them. If you hold them too much and tell them do this and that, they're going be stuck. Let them be free.

YOU CAN NEVER CHANGE THE KID. THE KID'S GOTTA CHANGE HIMSELF.

MAKE THE CHILD HAPPY AND TEACH THEM WITH SMILES.

Don't say, "I told you to do that, how many times!" Forget that because the child will not want to perform then. You don't want someone come at you and yell to do the stuff. So we joke a lot with the kids and their parents. We tell them, "Smile, because you're not in prison." And when the child does something good, you tell them, "That's it, you're getting there, you're getting there." If the kid does something that's not right, don't say that it's a bad habit. They're not bad habits, because nobody taught them the right way. Bad habits are when you teach them something and they still do it wrong.

Young kids are always looking for something, whether in a video, or a book, or an explanation, something easy that will make them good. They're dreaming. They want a perfect video, perfect disc. It doesn't work like that. They still need the patience and discipline to work and learn through repetition.

So, you have to do the drills a thousand times. Repetition, that's the way to learn a baseball skill.

YOU GOTTA TALK TO THE KIDS.

To understand what they're thinking and how they're feeling you have to talk and listen to the kids. You can lose everything if you only go by what you think. The kids remind us constantly that they are all individuals and when we begin to communicate individually with each one, with smiles, love and understanding, then the wealth of knowledge that we can share with them becomes unbelievable.

The ability to communicate with the kids is the key to teaching and learning that will bring about a positive measure of improvement very quickly. Once we learn how to communicate, then it becomes easy to teach the fundamental mechanics of baseball of throwing catching, fielding and hitting in an ABCDE, orderly method of application.

"I'M ALWAYS LEARNING SOMETHING FROM THE KIDS."

CHAPTER 7

A HUNDRED AND ONE STORIES

Those who know him personally will tell you that Manju Nitta is a great storyteller and has hundreds of stories. Herein are a few of them.

FRANCIS FUNAI

At age 42, I began "mind picking" people, all the good baseball coaches and greats, so that I could become a better coach. And so I called Mr. Francis Funai on the phone. "Mr. Funai you don't know me, but I'm Manju. You're the dean of fundamental baseball mechanics. You are the professor and I want to learn from you. So please teach me baseball." He said, "Thank you for the compliments but when do you want to learn." "Right now, I'm downstairs. Can I come up to the office?" "What? Oh! Okay." So I went up, went into the conference room.

Coach Funai always taught fundamental baseball mechanics step by step, sometimes so slowly that there were some who couldn't stand it. But he used to say, "You have to teach them how to walk before they can run."

He also told Manju, "Listen to what I say, but don't be me. Don't be a clone. Be yourself. Don't try to be me. Listen and learn from everybody, but be yourself."

GO FISHING

Early in his coaching career, Manju was helping Coach Francis Funai with the Iolani Baseball Team. During the first few weeks of tryouts they went up and down the many rows of young ball players, correcting their forms, explaining to them why they were doing this and that, suggesting better ways to perform and practice their baseball skills, etc. After a couple of weeks, Coach Funai told Manju, "I told five boys today to Go Fishing." Apparently this was something he had repeated over the years to youngsters who didn't seem dedicated to baseball.

Manju thought it sounded kind of funny, but didn't quite understand, so he asked Mr. Funai what he meant by "Go Fishing." Coach Funai told him, "You see, George, after many weeks of explaining and correcting some of the basic fundamentals and mechanics of baseball to the boys, if they still don't do them properly I tell them, 'Son, why don't you go fishing.' That way he doesn't bother me and I don't bother him.

A year later and the start of another season, Mr. Funai told Manju again that he told three boys to go fishing. Manju asked him, "Which three boys?" And when they were pointed out to him, Manju said, "I know those three boys, Mr. Funai." He looked surprised and thought that perhaps Manju knew those boys like family or friends. But Manju told him, "Where those boys live there is no water to go fishing. So can we bring them back and I will work with them some more?" Coach Funai smiled and said, "Sure, and you're funny George."

KEEP AN OPEN MIND

Mr. Funai had an open mind, even at age 80. One day when Manju was visiting with him, Mr. Funai was fretting because his 5-year-old granddaughter wanted to learn to play baseball. He thought that she was too young at which point Manju introduced him to the paper ball. With the paper ball his granddaughter was not going to get hurt. His mind was open, even at age 80.

You have to keep an open mind because unless you do, you're going to stop learning and then you can't teach.

STAN HASHIMOTO

Then I went to Stan Hashimoto. He knew about me because we were both from Waipahu, and he apparently knew how cocky and egotistical I was. "Stan, I was your mascot you know when you were 17 at Waipahu High School. You went to AJA, U.H., Hawaii League, Japan, etc. Can you show me some stuff?" He looked at me and said, "I don't know anything Manju." "Hey, no act like that, Stan. Show me some stuff!" "Don't you understand English, I don't know anything, I can teach you nothing. Look at me, nothing, you understand. 'No!'" So I was laughing on the inside because I was so cocky and egotistical and I believed him. I told myself, "Step aside you old man and I'll show you some stuff." So I told Stan, "Well let me show you some stuff." "Oh, you can show me some stuff, like throwing, fine. I'll look at you."

We went outside to the St. Andrews Priory parking lot nearby because his office was too small. He said, "Well start," so I do a throwing form. "How come you're so full of tension in your body. Look, your body's so tight, how are you going to throw? You're going get cramps." So I went into another form, a different form, a little more relaxed. Then he says, "Oh!" and he touches me and flips me right over. "How can you throw when you're off balanced, Manju?" "See you're falling down." "Oh!" I got up more mad, made another form. Half an hour, I went through all the forms I could think of, and he always would just touch me, "Oh you're still off balanced, tight over here yet." He never said that I was junk or that I was wrong. He destroyed me very pleasantly. He put a big mirror in front of me, to see myself, that's what it was. And after half an hour I gave up. I said, "Okay, thanks Stan," and I left.

I was totally depressed for two weeks. I told my wife, "I quit baseball. I don't want to hear, I don't want to see, I don't want to talk baseball. I don't know anything." But after a couple of weeks went by, I went back to see Stan. "Hey, Manju, what's up?" I told him I was totally depressed. He said, "What? Get in this office, get in the room," and he locked the door. "Get up, look at me, look at my eyes. Look at me and be the same person you were. Be the same Manju that you were; I didn't mean to put you down that deep." I said, "What do you mean?" He said, "I never can change your personality or your character. You're always going to be the same guy, but maybe your peripheral vision is going to be bigger now, your mind is going to be open. Before your mind was closed." He made me look at myself. It was as though he put a big mirror in front of me.

And that's how my association with Sensei Stan Hashimoto began. At age 44 I finally met my baseball sensei.

STAN'S PEARLS

When I first asked Stan how to teach baseball, he said, "You start like the alphabet, ABCDE. You start and stay in sequence. You don't start with A, then go to D or E and then come back to B. Always stay in sequence."

And when you see a problem in throwing the ball, catching or hitting, break it down, Manju, you break it down until you find the answer. Because if you can break it down, you'll find the answer.

"Oh, that's interesting, but how long do I continue to try to break down the problem if I can't find the answer?" He said, "What do you think?" I said, "One week?" "No." "One month?" "No." Two months sounds ridiculous, I'm thinking, so I said, "Three months?" "No." "Well, how long then?" "Infinitely, until you resolve the problem. And when you do, the kids are going to show it and you are going to be a most happy man."

"You have to look at the kid. Sometimes you have to step back and look at him from afar. Sometimes you have to look at him from the rear, or from the side. You have to look, you have to think, and if what you are thinking doesn't work, you have to throw it out the window. You think again, you look, you feel and try again. Sometimes you may be looking too hard and you have to look tomorrow. And keep on looking, infinitely." I thought, "Wow, that's exciting! Okay, I'm going to try that." And that's how I started.

See The Kids Improving? After a few years, Stan asked me, "Manju, when you're teaching the kids, do you see improvement?" I said, "Yeah, but sometimes not that much." All I'm asking is this. "Is there some improvement?" I said "Yeah." "Instant improvement?" "Yeah." "Then you're on the right track, so keep going. I know plenty of coaches who say the right words, Manju, a lot more beautifully than you, but if nothing happens to the kids, it doesn't mean a thing."

PROBLEM SOLVER

Every time I had a problem I went to see Stan. I'd explain the problem to him. But somehow eventually he always made me answer my own questions. "Well, what do you think?" "I think this and this." "Well, what's wrong with that?"

Stan, he makes me think!

NO RIGHT OR WRONG

Stan told him, there is no right or wrong in the way Manju was teaching. First of all, Manju says, "I have no degree in baseball," so people may not believe me anyway. Stan told him, "Just tell people that you are a farmer who likes baseball. Just tell people that you raise cucumber and nasubi, that's all. You know that what you're doing is working. Second, can you be right, right, right all your life? No. Why no? Are you perfect? No, you have plenty of faults. Who's the only perfect person? God. Whatever you do, you're going to fall sometimes. Whatever you do you're going to have disappointments, you're going to have failures. But remember, Manju, you're not going to fall like before, you're not going to fall hard and deep like you did before when you were so egotistical. You're going to fall, but you're going to come up; then you're going to go even higher. So keep going in your program because you've had success and the kids will keep coming to you. You're on the right track in baseball, so keep on going."

"By saying that I'm just a farmer who likes baseball, nobody will be attacking me. No one is questioning what I teach. I don't have to fight off anybody. I never say that my way is right and your way is wrong."

BE A GOOD LISTENER

He tells me you have to listen to people. I thought I was a good listener but I was wrong. One day I went to his office because I wanted to tell him something. But as soon as I sat down, he was yelling and screaming at me. My parents, they never appreciate me, Manju. Every Saturday I take them out riding and out for lunch. But they only grumble, grumble, grumble. They whine, whine, and whine. They just keep telling me how bad life is, and on and on. I'd like to say something but they won't listen." For half an hour Stan went on and on, cussing his parents, cursing them, and I just sat there. I asked myself, "My sensei, how can he be this kind of guy?" He was showing me the other side of his character. And after he was finished, he stood up and walked out. I sat there in total bewilderment, completely lost.

A couple of days later I went back to see him. He marches in and says, "Hey, thanks for listening, Manju. It was getting me down, and I wanted to get it off my chest.   No, I didn't want any advice. I knew what to do. Thank you." "Oh, Okay." So all I had to do was to listen.

THE KID WILL CHANGE HIMSELF

Stan told me that you can never change the kid. The kid's got to change himself. No matter what the coaches says, if the kid doesn't understand, he's still not going to do well. He's got to feel what you're talking about and what you're trying to teach. And when the kid starts to feel the thrill of throwing right or hitting the ball harder, he's going to change because he likes the feeling that comes with it.

The kids are the miracles. We, the coaches and their parents, are just part of the support system for them. The kids make themselves good.

EVERYTHING IS DONE BY FEELINGS

How are you going to teach a boy to feel something in baseball? Like sugar. How sweet is sugar? You know it's sweet, but how sweet is sugar? You have to taste it, then you'll know how sweet it is. That's why you have to make the kid taste it, make him feel it. You can't just tell the kid that this is the way to throw a ball or hit a ball. He's got to taste how good it is, to feel how good it is when he throws the ball right or to whack the ball solidly. And when the kid starts to get the feeling, then he's going to change because he likes that feeling. You've got to feel baseball. Until you feel baseball, you're not going to be good. That's why I tell parents and coaches, don't go grabbing the kids too much. Let them do it on their own because they're going to correct themselves. Just encourage. If you hold them too much and keep telling them, "Do this," and "Do that," they're going to get stuck. Let them be free.

USE THE MAGIC MIRROR IN YOUR BACK POCKET

If the ballplayer doesn't seem to be listening or doesn't seem to understand what you are talking about, or perhaps just looking at the bugs and flowers on the field, or looking at you and starting to cry, then you have to bring out that magic mirror in your back pocket. Slide it gently up to your face and look into it and give one big yell – Aaaahhgghh!!! The problem is not the ballplayer who is standing in front of you. He is waiting to be taught. It is you.

Then you must start all over again and look at the ballplayer with a great big smile and say, 'I love you,' and 'Thank you for coming.' Because if that ballplayer runs away and disappears, then you won't know whether what you are doing really works, whatever it may be. All the baseball knowledge that you have stored up in your brain may not amount to anything if there is no one to pass it to. You're going to be smart for nothing and only think that it may work.

DO IT WITH SMILES

You don't want someone coming at you screaming and yelling to do your thing. If the coach is constantly shouting, "How many times I told you to do 'em like this," that kid isn't likely to perform for you. We tell them smile because you're not in prison. And when the child does something good, tell them, "That's it, you're getting there, you're really getting there."

The Kid is the Miracle

As coaches, we are only a support system, encouraging them through their growth and performance. And as they improve, it is an infinitely rewarding feeling to be a part of their lives.

Don't Be A Quitter. It's too easy to quit!

"My Sensei Stan said that when you help people, all the goodness is going to come back to drown you."

Father Halter

I volunteered to help the Iolani School baseball program when my daughter started to go to school there and was assigned to assist Father Halter with the Intermediate School Team.

On my first day of practice Father Halter gave me a couple of sheets of paper and said that this will be the daily schedule of practice and that every day I would be getting a sheet of paper. On the sheet was written what time practice began and ended, and in between, the kind of baseball situations that would be needed to be addressed. After reading all this material, I decided to quit because I felt this very structured program was not for me. But when I talked to my sensei Stan Hashimoto, he said, "Father Halter is a good man, go and help him."

So I went back the following day, but helping Father was easier said than done because he took total control of everything and seemed to want no input from his assistant coaches. I decided to quit the team for the second time. But when I spoke to my Sensei Stan, he again looked at me and said, "Father Halter is a good man, go and help him."

I went back to the team and Father gave me another sheet of paper and said we have to perfect these situations before the season starts. But I felt that the baseball situations he wanted to practice were so simple and elementary, it was silly to practice them. I decided to quit for the third time. Once again I met my Sensei and told him how I felt about Father Halter's silly baseball situations. "He does not need my help and doesn't even ask for help."

At that point Stan said, "Manju, Father Halter has problems with the Head Master in regard to baseball, right?" I said, "Yes." "He has problems with the Athletic Director about his baseball program, right?" "Yes." "He has problems with the Varsity coach who runs the entire baseball program, right?" "Yes." "He has problems with all the parents of his team, right?" "Yes." "And he has problems with all the players on his team, right?" "Yes." "Then, Manju, why are you thinking of giving him one more problem?"

I went back to the team and for the next three years I did not give Father Halter any problems. I just helped him.

Father Halter was a great person. He was a priest, a teacher and a student of baseball. He cured me of swearing on the ball field. He didn't know too much about fundamental baseball mechanics, so every time a kid did something wrong he would say, "What is wrong with the boy? Look at him George. Go talk to him."

Jeffrey was a centerfielder who always seemed lackadaisical and stood in the field as though nothing mattered, as though he didn't have a care in the world. And all the shouting and yelling by Father Halter didn't seem effective. So I was asked to talk to him. I asked him, "Jeff, are you giving us 100% of your effort?" "Oh, yes." he says. I told him, "Take a look across the canal. KC Drive-Inn over there is going to close tomorrow and they're going to give a bonanza, a huge banana split for only 5 cents. I want you to make believe that I'm your best friend and you have to convince me that we should go get the banana split before they close. Okay?" So Jeff begins, "Coach, KC Drive-Inn is going to give out banana splits with all the trimmings for five cents so we have to go." Meanwhile I had turned around and was looking in the opposite direction, paying no attention to Jeff. Then I turned back and said, "Convince me, Jeff. What's the matter with you? I'm your best friend and I love ice cream." So he started talking again, and I turned away again. "Jeff, you're not convincing me. What's wrong Jeff?" He said, "Coach, you're not listening!" I said, "What?" "You're not listening, Coach!" "So what about it? Do you feel like talking if I'm not listening? Well, when the coach is talking and you're not paying attention and listening out in the field, now you know what he's feeling, yeah. Go out there and don't do that again." He was fine after that.

Mark, the leftfielder, seemed to have a lot of trouble moving to the balls on either side so Father asked me to talk to him. I told him, "Mark, Father is very unhappy with you. Are you giving us 100%?" "Oh, yes, 125%" "Father says that you cannot move left or right. How long have you been playing in the outfield?" "First year, Coach. I was playing in the infield all this time." "Oh, no wonder. We've never taught you the left and right clearance drills, the outfield drills. Come on." For the next hour I showed him the drills. I went back and showed Father how he could move.   Father Halter turned to me and said, "Thank you, George."

Scott was a straight A student. One day, just before the start of the season, he told Father Halter that he was thinking of quitting the team. Father told me that the boy needs help, so I cornered Scott. "What's this? Three more days before the season starts and you're our starting right fielder and you're going to quit. Why?" "Because I never got a fair chance this year. Last year you taught us the entire infield drills, and I though I was pretty good." "Yes, you were, but Father wants you in the outfield." "But I didn't get a fair chance playing the infield this year." I told him, "Okay, Scott, for the next three days I'm going to try you out at second base. I'm going to hit you grounders, double play balls, everything. You show Father Halter what you've got, and when we're finished, will you concur with whatever Father tells you to do?" So after the third day, we asked Father what he thought. Father said, "You're going to be my right fielder." Scott said, "Yes, Coach," took off to the outfield and we had no problems afterward.

MORE OF MANJU'S STORIES

KEEP ON LOOKING

Jerry was a CPA who had brought his son to the clinics. After a few sessions he asked me to teach him, the father, how to throw because he had never played ball and wanted to be able to practice with his son. So we went through the throwing drills, slowly and thoroughly, but for some reason he couldn't throw straight. His balls were usually up in the air or down in the ground, and this despite one-on-one sessions lasting up to one and a half hours, twice a week. I looked at him from near, from far, from the side, from the back and from the front as Jerry threw ball after ball into a net. Many times both Jerry and I were frustrated, but I said, we're going to keep looking until we find the answer. I tried many different avenues because the ones that I was trying didn't work. I was disappointed with myself and felt that something must be wrong with me. I was almost ready to give up.

However, finally after almost six months of twice weekly sessions, half a year, I saw something. Jerry did all the drills correctly, including the crank and step, pull and kick, etc., but somehow, just before releasing the ball, something went askew. And then I saw it. When Jerry pulled his left arm around and back, the hand and glove was facing up, toward the sky. His left forearm was supinated and this prevented the full release of his shoulders. Once he got rid of that habit and began to pull his left arm and hand correctly, around and back, he could throw straight and true, right at the target. It took a long time, but Jerry made me realize that my mind cannot be closed. He literally opened my mind.

MICHAEL, THE TREE CLIMBER

This lady brought her 10-year-old daughter and 5-year-old Michael to the clinic when I first began baseball clinics at Ala Moana Park many years ago. His sister loved the baseball clinics but Michael always climbed up a small banyan tree behind the scoreboard and stayed there all afternoon, until his sister and mother were ready to go home. His mother would always encourage him to come down. "Your turn, Michael," but he wouldn't come down from the tree. I told her, "Don't force him. He has to come down on his own terms." This went on every Sunday afternoon, for almost a year.

Then one Sunday, I told him "Michael, your turn. Come," and the boy started to come down from the tree. "Hey, everybody, look Michael's coming down from the tree." All the kids cheered for him. He finally put on his glove and said he wanted to learn the baseball drills. But from the beginning, he knew exactly what to do. All that time, from his perch up in the tree, he had been watching and listening and, finally, he felt confidant in his ability to perform well enough to start to play ball.

The most important thing he taught me was that it was his choice when to come down from that tree, when to let us know that he wanted to play baseball. All we had to do was just wait until he was ready.

PATIENCE

One day, after one of our clinics, this man came over and asked me to help his son, a chubby eight-year-old boy. He said, "Coach, my son wants to play baseball but he never played at all. Do you think you can help him?" I said, sure, he could come to one of our regular clinics, but the father wanted me to teach the boy something now. I looked at his son and asked him, "Do you want to learn to play baseball?" He nodded yes with a shy smile. So I began working with the kid that afternoon. But as we were preparing to begin some throwing drills, his father took off to join his friends who were drinking on the hillside.

After an hour or so of working with the boy, I decided to call it quits, and the father came trotting back. He shook my hand, patted me on my back and said "Manju, thank you so much. What a guy! You're so patient, you're terrific." I replied, "What does patience got to do with it?" The startled father stepped back. Then he said, "I said patient, because for an hour you worked with my son and I was watching you."

I was quite angry. "First of all you told me to help your son, right? But then you abandoned him and took off to go drinking with your gang. Your boy wanted you to be right here with him. Your son is trying to learn baseball to please you and hope that you'd be proud of him. I spent an hour with him today and I'm willing to help him forever, but patience has nothing to do with it. So don't ever abandon him again."

Sometimes they just can't see what their kids need.

HAVING FUN

This schoolteacher brought her 10-year-old son to the Sunday clinics for about a year. She always sat under a tree, seemingly reading her books but watching her son on the side. One Sunday I decided to test her to see if she was really serious about her son's baseball progress.

I told the boy, "We're going to have some fun today, okay? You see your mom over there. Well, in the next ten minutes she's going to come over here and she's going to yell and scream at you. You're not going to do anything wrong but just play with me because your mom is very observant." So I had him hit the ball and whack! He hits the ball. But then I made a cockeyed face and he starts laughing as he tries to swing at the ball. Then I pushed my nose up and eyelids down, and again the boy could hardly swing the bat because he was laughing so hard. When Mom saw this, she ran up to him and said, "What's wrong with you, son, laughing and wasting Coach's time. I feel like whacking you!" The boy continued laughing and I said, "See, what I told you?" Mom says, "What do you mean? What happened?" "We were just play acting. I knew you were watching intently. I told him you were going to come over here to scold him, but you went total with him, yeah." So we learned that most parents watch their kids very intently, during practice as well as during games.

LAUGH WITH HIM, BUT NOT AT HIM

This father asked me if I could help his son who was somewhat handicapped. I said sure, try bring him and perhaps he'll enjoy doing what we do. So he brought this 12-year-old, good-looking boy. The boy went through the drills and not infrequently he would drop the ball when he was throwing and miss the balls that came his way. But he was having fun and laughing all the time and everyone was laughing with him. The parents were watching from a good distance, and afterwards, the father came. "Excuse my son yeah, Coach." I said, "Hey, nothing to be excused. I'm going to let your son have fun. Maybe he's not going to be the best ball player, but he can have fun and at least he's going to learn something. The other kids had a lot of fun with him. I told them they can laugh with him, but nobody laughs at him. So what's wrong with that? And why were you watching from so far away? Were you ashamed of your son? I wasn't." They brought the kid back a few times after that.

No "Negatives" at Our Clinics

This doctor, who brought his son to our clinics, was a rather strict disciplinarian. One day he was upset because the son wasn't performing well.

Finally, he told his son that he was going to whack him if he didn't do the drills right. At that point I had to tell him, "Don't ever hit him in front of me. If you want to hit him, take him home. I've told you, here we allow no "negatives". You can take all the pictures you like but no negatives. That includes no swearing and no yelling at the kids. If I cry, you're in trouble, and I cry very easily." There are a lot of other kids around and if the adults act like that, the other kids are going to be intimidated too.

Remember The Kid's Name

Who's this kid now? This boy says, "You keep forgetting my name, Coach, and I've been coming for three months." He scolded me, because it seemed as though "You don't know who I am, Coach?" And, sure enough, when I started calling him by his name, he became alive. His attitude changed, his posture changed, he started to listen more because I had acknowledged him with his name now. The kids, they're the ones who teach us.

Ed "Soupy" Kawawaki

He is well known in Honolulu as a premier massage therapist and sports trainer. He was a University of Hawaii football star in the mid-50s and was the quarterback on the famous Rainbow team that upset the powerful University of Nebraska 6-0, at Nebraska. He taught sports medicine for many years at Leeward Community College and asked Coach Manju to teach a course on baseball drills 20 years ago. It was then that he introduced Manju to "paper balls" which could be thrown around in the classroom. Paper balls are made with a base of newspaper, which is crunched into the size of a baseball, then wrapped in athletic "pre-tape," and a final wrap of two-inch wide, regular tape. These paper balls are perfect for four, five and six-year old kids who are first learning to field and catch balls without getting hurt.

REHABILITATING A TRIPLE-A PITCHER

Soupy called Manju to help this guy who had a sore arm. The arm was better now, but he still couldn't throw. It was then that Manju met Joey Vierra who had been a star at the University of Hawaii and was in professional baseball at the triple A level. He got hurt pitching. "How did you get hurt, Joey?" He was told to get rid of his long kick with men on bases; told to quick pitch. You can't do that. You have to ankle crank when you slide step. Without a crank the arm "detaches" and you'll develop a sore arm again. How can I help him? Oh yes, the split drill!! First pull and kick. Hit my hand; then hit where my hand was. That's where you have to release. 6 weeks. What a beautiful experience.

BLISTERS AND SORE ARMS

No one's supposed to get blisters. You have to figure why the kid is having blisters. Oftentimes it's because he was turning the bat over while swinging. Similarly, when the ball player gets hurt, you have to find out why. If they have pain in the arm or shoulder, the pain will recur unless you find out why he's getting the pain. If the throwing mechanics continue improperly, he will get a sore arm again. Throw properly and you won't get hurt.

"MAKE MY SON AN ALL-STAR"

A coach brought his 10-year-old son to me at Ala Moana Park where we were conducting our regular Sunday baseball clinics. He said, "Can you make my son an all-star baseball player?" I looked at him in amazement and said, "I'm sorry but I don't make any child an all-star player. You brought him to the wrong place. Only God and your son himself can make him an all-star player." He said, "Okay then, can you teach him all of the things you're doing?" I said, "Of course."

Within a year his son learned a lot of baseball skills and was voted an all-star player at the end of the season. Tournament games started but in the championship game his son made three errors and the game was lost. The next day he brought his son to the park and told me about his disappointment and embarrassment at his son's performance. "How can he make all those errors when he has been learning all of the baseball skills for a year?"

I told him nobody wants to make any errors but the father continued to be angry and said a few more negative things about his son. When he finally settled down I asked him, "Are you finished?" He sort of mumbled and said, "Yes." I said please look at your son while I do the talking. I asked him, "Do you believe your son wanted to make three errors in front of you?" He said "No!" "Then why are you scolding him? Do you think he wanted to make those errors in front of his teammates and his coaches?" He said "No." "Then why are you on his case. Do you think he wanted to make those errors in front of all the parents, in front of grandma and grandpa?" He said, "No." "Then look at your son straight in the eye and say, I'm very sorry."

"Now let's talk a little baseball about the game. What position was he in when he made those three errors?" He said, "I don't know." "What kind of ball did he miss when he made those three errors? Was it a regular bounce, a high choppy bounce, or the ones that just slows down and spins crazily?" He said he didn't know. I said, "I have to know because we have to show him how to catch those balls so he doesn't make those errors again. Look at your son again and please say you love him. Because we're talking about baseball and it's only a game."

BRINGING THE OLD COACH BACK

After a baseball clinic for coaches and parents, we were enjoying some doughnuts and coffee when an energetic young man approached me and shook my hand. He said he learned so much this evening and that he was ready to get on the field and "go for it." Then he added that it was good that he got rid of the former coach who was old and didn't know anything. When he said that, I almost choked on my doughnut. I put my coffee down, shook the young man's hand and said, "Son, are you that good?" He looked at me and said, "No, but the old man was worse." This time I took both of his hands, looked at his eyes and, a little louder than before, said, "Son, are you that good?" He said, "No, I'm just learning." I said, "Do me a big favor.

Call the old coach tonight and ask him to be the head coach again." He said, "No, I cannot do that." I looked at him again and said, "Son, are you that good?" This time he looked back at me and said, "Okay, I'm going to call him tonight."

After a couple of days, I went down to the practice field to see my young friend. He said he called the old coach and asked him to come back to be the head coach, but the old man refused. I thanked this young coach for the big favor he did for me. Then I asked him whether the old coach had a grandson playing on the team. He said, "Yes." I asked him when he kicked the old coach out of the team, where was he watching the game from. He said, "Out in centerfield, far away." "After you told him to come back, where is he watching the game from now? He said, "Near the dugout." I hugged the young coach and thanked him for everything. He said he didn't do anything. I smiled at him before leaving and said, "Yes, you did. You allowed a grandpa to watch his grandson up close again, and another thing, son." He asked, "What?" I told him "You are that good!"

TOO SHY TO LEARN

A mom brought her six-year-old son to our clinic and introduced him to me but he was very shy and wrapped himself around her mom's leg and wouldn't let go until I left to help some other kids. He would play toss and catch with his mom but would wrap himself around mom whenever I appeared. They came to the clinic for half a dozen Sundays but he would not let go of mom so I thought that perhaps he was not ready for baseball. Then suddenly, one Sunday, he came and sat down beside me as I was working with another young boy. After I finished with the boy, I looked at him and said, "It's your turn, son." When he stood up with his glove I asked him, "How many times do you want to throw to me", and he said "50 times." So I rolled the ball to him and he threw every ball right into my glove, 50 times." I didn't attempt to teach him anything because I wanted him to be comfortable and since I finally got him to let go of his mom.

I told him let's go hit the ball into the net and asked, "How many times do you want to hit the ball. He said 50 times, so I tossed the ball to him and he swung 50 times, and although he contacted the ball only around five times, he was drenched with sweat but never gave up until he swung the bat 50 times. I shook his hand and said, "Great job. That's enough for today, but I'll see you next Sunday, huh?"

The following Sunday, I asked him how many times he wanted to throw the ball, to which he replied, "80 times." So he threw every ball right into my glove 80 times. Then when he went to the batting net, he said he wanted to hit the ball 80 times. I asked him, "Do you want to swing 80 times or do you want to hit the ball 80 times. He said, "Hit the ball." I said loudly, "Why didn't you tell me earlier that you wanted to hit the ball. I though you just wanted to show me how you swing." "Okay then, here is what you have to do to have a level swing, here is what you have to do to contact the ball, here is what you need to have power to drive the ball." And when I tossed the ball to him, he contacted the ball probably 70 times in 80 swings." At the end of the session I don't know who was happier, the mom or the boy.

So once again this shy youngster taught me to open my mind further. I thanked him for teaching me, and he smiled at me not really knowing what I meant.

MAKING THE TEAM (OR THE START OF THE BASEBALL SEASON)

Every new baseball season means tryouts, followed by cutting the team to size, a very traumatic time for many kids. Invariably there are heartaches and headaches and disgruntled parents who can't understand why their sons did not make the ball team. So after a few years, Coach Manju and his fellow coaches instilled a new, three week, pre-season clinic of baseball drills including throwing, catching, fielding, running, and batting for the Iolani Intermediate School team. Every baseball candidate went through three weeks of learning and practicing the basic fundamentals and mechanics of baseball, and at the end of that period they were all asked to go through a day of testing.

A five point system was created for the five basic baseball skills – throwing, catching and fielding, running and batting. All six coaches judged and awarded points to every candidate for all the baseball skills. The points were added up and those with the highest number of points made the team and the others were dropped. Those who were released were spoken to individually. They were thanked for their hard work, encouraged to try out again the following year. They were told where their weaknesses were and encouraged to seek help in order to improve.

LEFT–HANDERS IN THE INFIELD

In sandlot baseball and softball games it is not unusual to see a left-handed fielder playing in any position in the infield. However, when one gets into a higher and more competitive level of the game, it is easy to see that the left-handed third baseman, shortstop or second baseman has a definite handicap in fielding and throwing to first or second base because he has to pivot hard or make a 360 degree turn before he throws. The reason coaches put the left hander in those positions is that the player may be the best athlete and they do not know how to train others to play in the positions.

Coach Manju learned of this problem when a young softball player who had been coming to his Sunday clinics for a number of years, returned with her parents and they all had a disappointed look. The parents said that she was having a hard time fielding and throwing the ball. Yet when Manju checked her fundamental baseball mechanics, she was fine.

So he asked her what position did her coaches have her playing. She said, "Shortstop." Manju smiled at her and jokingly said, "Oh, that's wonderful. Please make all the errors you want because it is not your fault." He explained to her and her parents that left-handers shouldn't play in the infield other than first base because of the nature of the game. He suggested they talk to the head coach if she could try out for a position as a first baseman or outfielder.

She did find a position in the outfield, did very well, and at the end of the softball season she was selected the OIA Player of the Year.

FINALLY, MORE OF MANJU

If you don't acknowledge those around you, you're not going to have them help you. I don't care if they're good or not good. But when you start treating everyone with respect, and they don't have to be ball players, then lots of things are going to happen. They're going to come and help you in their own way, perhaps hustling for money, making kaukau for you, etc. No matter what the circumstances, I usually learn something.

Even if only one person asks, I'll come and perform and teach if they ask me to.

On Teaching and Learning: No matter how much a teacher knows, if the pupil doesn't learn, the teacher has failed. Success is when learning has transpired.

You have to do it a thousand times. Practice, practice, practice, that's what makes you good.

My life is centered around baseball and baseball has been good to me. All the good things that have happened to me have been because of baseball.

CHAPTER 8

COACH AND TEACHER
GEORGE "MANJU" NITTA

The kids call him Coach Nitta and his assistants call him Coach Manju, but they should be calling him Teacher or "*Sensei*" because that's what he really is. George "Manju" Nitta has been teaching basic baseball principles to kids of all ages for more than 35 years, and they keep flocking to his free clinics to learn the basics of baseball from the master. His "Sunday Schools," held every Sabbath afternoon almost all year round, and presently at the Beretania Community Park, is the best thing around for baseball aspirants of all ages and children in particular. Certainly there is no better bargain in town. His clinics are free!

His parents owned a small bakery/restaurant and Manju (a type of Japanese bean-jam bun)

George "Manju" Nitta

acquired his nickname very early. [One of his brothers was nicknamed *Anpan* (another type of Japanese pastry) and another was called *Dango* (a Japanese dumpling)].

Manju fell in love with baseball at an early age. The bakery/restaurant was located on Waipahu's Depot Road, just a stone's throw from Hans L'Orange Park where the mighty Waipahu team of the Rural AJA (Americans of Japanese Ancestry) League played. He became the team mascot at age 10 and found a host of idols and heroes among the perennial champions of the Rural League. By the time he was a teenager he was busy playing in the Waipahu Amateur League, and then with the Waipahu High School's championship teams.

After high school he joined the Army to learn a trade, but the Army found that he was too valuable as a ball player, and baseball is what he did for three years while in uniform. Upon discharge, he turned professional and played for the Hiroshima Carps' farm team in Japan. However, his Japanese professional career was cut short by an injury in his second year. Upon his return to Hawaii, his old Waipahu High School mentor, Masa Yonamine, asked him to play for Asahi of the Hawaii Baseball League (HBL). Asahi won the crown in five of the eight years that Manju played for them. Then he was asked to manage and coach the Ujimori Hawks, the team that replaced the Rural Red Sox in the HBL, which he did for the next ten years.

Despite all the years of playing baseball, he says he really did not know much about the game until he was able to "open his mind" and began "*mind-picking*" the experts of the game. This was a gradual and sometimes painful process, but along the way, he learned to break down the basics of baseball -- throwing, fielding and hitting the ball -- down to its components and put them back together in the proper sequences. To be effective, all athletic acts have to have the components put together in the proper sequence.

His "*sensei*" was the legendary Stan Hashimoto who starred for the University of Hawaii, Waipahu's AJA team, Rural Red Sox, and the Toei Flyers and Taiyo Whales in the Japanese Professional League. Stan was Manju's teacher, counselor and advisor. And since age 42, Manju has continued the legacy of another baseball legend, the late Coach Francis Funai, teaching the basics of baseball to any and all who are willing to learn.

Coach Ruth Komatsu and Protégé

Except for the month of December, Manju holds baseball clinics at the Beretania Community Park every Sunday afternoon from 1 to 5 p.m. Invariably, there are a dozen and more neophytes, usually kids four to ten years old, who come to learn the basics of baseball. The "veterans," usually older kids from ten to eighteen, come a bit later, around 2:30 p.m., to do the drills and learn the finer points of the game. By the end of the day, there have been some three dozen kids and their parents who have come to the park. Some of the kids keep coming back for weeks, months and even years.

At first Manju used to run the drills and clinics alone. Over the years he's had a few disciples who have been swept by his enthusiasm for the game and love of the kids, and they have joined him at his clinics. A few years ago Will Hoover wrote a beautiful article on him in the Honolulu Advertiser, and, as a consequence, Manju was quickly inundated by calls from eager parents of potential ball players. After Hoover's article, Manju found that he needed his "helpers," his "gang," his disciples, because his calendar was being constantly filled with requests to conduct baseball clinics. Two of his most faithful assistants are schoolteacher Ruth Komatsu and engineer Ken Sakai.

Coach Ken Sakai

In addition to his Sunday afternoon clinics, he frequently conducts one to three-day clinics from Waimanalo to Manoa, from Kaneohe to Wahiawa and in-between. He also makes annual or biannual visits to Hilo and Maui, and more recently to Molokai and Kauai. He has given a clinic in California and one of his disciples, a woman, is the guru of baseball clinics in the San Francisco Bay area.

So at age 74 and although completely retired from his job with the Building Department of the City, Manju is a very busy man, totally dedicated to the kids, and still filled with unimaginable enthusiasm and passion for the game of baseball. His dedication is complete and total. He'll make time for any kid and/or parent for special coaching above and beyond his clinics. All they have to do is just to call him or talk to him.

Somewhere along the line and some years ago, he came to the conclusion that baseball is what his life is all about and that teaching baseball to kids of all ages what he was born to do. He's found his mission and he is completely at peace with himself.

BIBLIOGRAPHY

1. *Baseball Clinic for Kiddies*. (Sports Camera Magazine, June, 1953.)

2. Ohira, Rod: *Funai Is A Diamond Legend*. (Honolulu Star Bulletin, 12-3-88).

3. Ohira, Rod: *At 84, This Baseball Guru Still is Learning New Tricks*. (Honolulu Star Bulletin, 3-12-91.)

4. Bob Shaw: *The Basic Fundamentals and Mechanics of Successful Pitching*. (The Viking Press, Inc., 625 Madison Ave., New York, N.Y. 10022, 1972).

5. Ted Williams and John Underwood: *The Science of Hitting*. (Simon and Schuster, New York, N.Y., 1986.)

6. Charley Lau Jr., with Jeffrey Flanagan: *Lau's Laws on Hitting*. (Addax Publishing Group Inc; Lenexa, KS 66215.)

7. Jerry Kindall: *Baseball: Play The Winning Way*. (Sports Illustrated Books, Lanham, MD 20706, 1993.)

8. Jeff Burrough: Little League Instructional Guide. (Bonus Books, Inc., Chicago 60611, 1994.)

9. Pat Jordan: *Pitching*. (Harpers & Row, Publishers, Inc., 10 East 53rd St., NY 10022, 1985.)

10. Robert K. Adair: *The Physics of Baseball*. (Harper-Collins Publishers Inc., NY, 10022, 1990.)

11. Don Marsh: *101 Things You Can Teach Your Kids About Baseball*. (Campbell Marsh Communications. 5010 Caminito Exquisito, San Diego, CA 92130-2850, 1990.)

12. Dusty Baker, Jeff Mercer, Marv Bittinger: *You Can Teach Hitting*. (Masters Press. 4255 West Touhy Avenue, Lincolnwood, Chicago, Ill. 60712-1975, 1993.)

13. Joe Morgan: *Baseball My Way*. (Halliday Lithograph Corporation. West Hanover and Plympton, Mass. 1976.)

ACKNOWLEDGEMENTS

George Manju Nitta wishes to thank the following people who have made his Baseball Dreams come true.

HIS TEACHERS

Father Halter of Iolani School
Masa Yonamine
Jack Ladra
Ben Ronquilio
Richard Nagamine
Ed Kawawaki
Michael and Carol Jean Kimura
Ken and Grace Kimura
Eddie and Ruth Uemori

FELLOW COACHES AT MANJU'S CLINICS

Art and Marsha Miyataki
Ruth Komatsu
Ken Sakai
Arnold Tamane
Dennis Fukunaga
Jim Miyake (Hilo)
Les Nakama (Maui)
Bob Kawaguchi (Maui)
Dennis Fukunaga

HIS FAMILY

Ruby E. Nitta
Misty and Nicholas Yee
Kainoa and Sophia Yee